Let's Read Together

Let's Read Together

BOOKS FOR FAMILY ENJOYMENT

Fourth Edition

Let's Read Together Revision Committee
Association for Library Service to Children
American Library Assocation

American Library Association
Chicago 1981

Library of Congress Cataloging in Publication Data

Association for Library Service to Children. Let's Read Together Revision Committee.
  Let's read together.

  First-3d ed. by the Special Committee of National Congress of Parents and Teachers and the Children's Services Division, American Library Association.
  Includes index.
  1. Children's literature—Bibliography. I. Special Committee of the National Congress of Parents and Teachers and the Children's Services Division, American Library Association. Let's read together. II. Title.
Z1037 A87 1981 [PN1009.A1] 010 80-39957
ISBN 0-8389-3253-3

Printed in the United States of America

Contents

Preface
to the Fourth Edition

While the number of children's books published is proportionately small compared to those produced for adults, nearly 3,000 new children's titles published annually can be overwhelming to parents seeking just the right books for the family sharing. This is also a problem for other adults seeking books to read aloud to children — in childcare centers, in classrooms, in church school programs, in libraries, on playgrounds, and around campfires.

This fourth edition of *Let's Read Together* contains many selections published during the past decade as well as a number of selections cited in the previous three editions. Equal attention was given to retain those timeless books that have been favorites of generations of children and to updating the bibliography with contemporary books that are well on their way to becoming classics in their own time. Also included are picture books that can be shared with the prereading child — some with simple texts and some significant wordless books. Books for older children reflect our changing society—the diversity of its ethnic composition, its family structures, and its growing respect for the differences as well as the commonalities that unite us.

Some section headings have been changed for this revision and books have been arranged alphabetically by title under each category. Some notable changes involve the omission of Special Days and the creation of a section entitled Celebrations. Sing-Aloud Books is a new category, and Guides to Children's Books has become Other Resources for Parents' Reading. Several sections have been expanded, notably Picture Books and Family Stories, in which category is now included the former Books for Family Sharing. No attempt has been made to provide an appendix of series books as before, because the list would be too lengthy. However, whenever a cited book is part of a series, this fact is noted in the annotation. The wider availability of paperback editions also is indicated wherever possible.

The committee agrees with Frances Sullivan who observed in the "Foreword to Parents" for the 1957–59 edition that "Ages given on the book jacket or in a graded list can indicate only in a general way the age or grade level for any book." This bibliography therefore provides some broad age and grade designations. Where the subject matter or level of sophistication suggests that the book is for an older listener, the annotations further indicate this. (*See* key to age/grade designations.)

Since price ranges change so frequently and availability of trade and paperback editions varies, book prices have been omitted. Parents are encouraged to borrow these books from their local libraries and to inquire at their local bookstores, should they wish to purchase particular books. The books listed in this fourth edition were in print as of early 1980.

The Revision Committee was comprised of members of the Association for Library Services to Children, a division of the American Library Association. In making their selections, some drew from their personal experiences as parents and all relied on the professional knowledge and judgment gained as working librarians in daily touch with children, parents, and teachers. The committee acknowledges with gratitude the support, advice, and practical assistance offered by colleagues and friends during the course of their work on this revision.

BARBARA ROLLOCK, CHAIR
ALSC *Let's Read Together* Revision
Committee (ad hoc)

HARRIET QUIMBY, EDITOR
CAROLYN JENKS
GINNY M. KRUSE
FRANCES SEDNEY
NAN STURDIVANT

Foreword
to Parents

"There is no substitute for books in the life of a child," says Mary Ellen Chase in her book, *Recipe for a Magic Childhood.* "The first understanding of this simple and irrefutable truth must come from his early perception of his parents' faith in it. They alone can give him his knowledge. . . ."

For families who love books and enjoy read-aloud sessions there is nothing so much worth doing as tasting, testing, and savoring all kinds of books. This sharing starts as soon as a small baby will listen to *Mother Goose;* progresses through the difficult stage when the books the children can read are not nearly so exciting and desirable as those you read to them; and goes on to the time when the young ones become as tall as their parents, and the sharing consists of recommending books to one another and the reading aloud of choice bits.

Finding the right book for reading aloud to one child, or to several children of different ages, as well as helping children select books from a library or bookstore are difficult for many parents. Children of the same age and grade level often vary greatly in their reading ability; children in the same family may have widely divergent interests and skills; and even the same child is likely to read at many levels. One beginning reader will take a longer time than another to move from *Little Bear* by Else H. Minarik to a book like *This Time, Tempe Wick?* by Patricia Gauch, which is difficult for some children in the third grade. Interest is a great spur to reading. Many beginning readers have little difficulty with the long names of prehistoric animals because these are words they want to know and recognize. For these reasons ages given on the book jacket or in a graded list can indicate only in a general way the interest or reading level for any book. Books in this list have been placed in age ranges covering several years. These ranges reflect interest and comprehension levels, *not* the reading level of the text. Selecting books for a particular child, or children, is made even more difficult—and interesting—because of the great number of juvenile books published each year.

Book lists, such as this one prepared by a committee of librarians, provide one means of selection. There is no magic in a book list that will guarantee a love of reading to any child. The magic is in the books themselves. When parents who have special knowledge concerning their own chidren work with librarians who know many books and many children, the finding of the right book is more likely to occur. Reading pleasure is made up of three parts—searching for the book, reading the book, and then sharing the book with someone else. Parents play an important role in all three steps.

Few things stimulate a love of reading more than the ownership of even a few well-loved books. There should be a place in the family budget for books—books for birthdays, for Christmas, and for other festive occasions. Some of these titles children themselves should have a part in selecting and purchasing. Gift-buying relatives will appreciate a list of books that children really want to own—books they have borrowed from the library and will read and use again and again, as well as additional titles by favorite authors. Books which have remained popular over a long period of time, such as *The Jungle Book,* are often published by more than one publishing house. These books will differ in price, design, and illustrator. Parents, and children, should examine the various editions at the library or bookstore before making a choice for their own library.

Knowing the author, title, and publisher for the books you wish to buy will make their purchase easier for you and will be helpful to the bookseller, who can order the books if they are not in stock. If there is no store selling books where you live, ask a librarian at the nearest public library or your state library agency for the address of stores nearest you. Because book prices are subject to change without notice, they have not been included in this edition.

Many parents have questions concerning the purchase of encyclopedias, other home reference books, and literary sets for children. Their purchase depends largely on the family budget and whether or not the family is a "that's interesting, let's look up more information" kind of family. Before buying anything as expensive as a set of encyclopedias, it is wise to look up the review of these sets in *Booklist*, published by the American Library Association. Consult your school, public, or state library for these reviews. Useful home reference books are included in this publication. The purchase of a set of books containing the different kinds of stories and poems children like and excerpts from books is an individual matter, depending in great part on whether or not the book budget can include both a set of books and individual titles. A set *cannot* take the place of favorite books.

The titles that follow have been chosen to help parents select with greater confidence books for family reading aloud, books for individual reading, and books for a child's own library. Some of them are useful to satisfy current interests and less advanced abilities; others have a timeless quality that provide a family literary heritage of knowledge, truth, laughter, inspiration, and beauty.

This "Foreword to Parents" by Frances Sullivan from the 1959 edition is reprinted again because it speaks so cogently to parents, the people for whom this bibliography is intended. Only minor revisions have been made to reflect changes in bibliographic format within the volume.

Key to Symbols

To assist users of this guide in determining approximate age and grade interest levels, the following symbols have been included. In some cases, where the appeal extends to a broader age range, a combination of symbols has been used.

- (A) Preschool through Grade 2, Ages 3-7
  - (★) Ages 1½-2
- (B) Grades 3 through 5, Ages 8-10
- (C) Grades 6 and 7, Ages 11-12
- (D) Grades 8 and up, Ages 13+

Nursery Rhymes
and Mother Goose

The Baby's Lap Book, comp. and illus. by Kay Chorao. Dutton, 1977. Wispy, nostalgic illustrations accompany these old familiar rhymes. (★A)

Book of Nursery and Mother Goose Rhymes, comp. and illus. by Marguerite de Angeli. Doubleday, 1954. Paper, Doubleday/Zephyr. Illustrations in soft colors and in black and white appear on every page of this bounteous collection. (A-B)

Brian Wildsmith's Mother Goose: A Collection of Nursery Rhymes, illus. by Brian Wildsmith. Watts, 1965. Paper, Watts. Familiar verses are illustrated on each page in bold, glowing watercolors. (A)

Cakes and Custards: Children's Rhymes, sel. by Brian W. Alderson; illus. by Helen Oxenbury. Morrow, 1975. A well-balanced collection which includes some of the compiler's childhood favorites as well as many traditional rhymes. Illustrated with wit, vigor, and superb draftsmanship. (A-B)

Father Fox's Pennyrhymes, by Clyde Watson; illus. by Wendy Watson. Crowell, 1971. Paper, Scholastic. These original verses have the lilt and rhythm of traditional folklore. (A-B)

Grandfa' Grig Had a Pig and Other Rhymes without Reason from Mother Goose, comp. and illus. by Wallace Tripp. Little, 1976. Paper, Little. The rhymes are old and familiar, but the detailed pictures add new and choice bits of humor. (A-B)

Hector Protector, and As I Went Over the Water: Two Nursery Rhymes with Pictures, illus. by Maurice Sendak. Harper, 1965. Two less familiar verses are enlarged upon by the raffish charm of Sendak's pictures. (A-B)

The House That Jack Built, illus. by Rodney Peppé. Delacorte, 1970. The cumulative rhyme is illustrated with brightly colored pictures, from Jack's house to the "cock that crowed in the morn." (A-B)

If All the Seas Were One Sea, illus. by Janina Domanska. Macmillan, 1971. Etchings in striking color illustrate this single rhyme. (A)

It's Raining, Said John Twaining: Danish Nursery Rhymes, tr. and illus. by N. M. Bodecker. A Margaret K. McElderry Book/Atheneum, 1973. Paper, Atheneum/Aladdin. Perky, rhythmic verses with a humorous quality that is echoed in the illustrations. (A-B)

The Mother Goose Book, illus. by Alice and Martin Provensen. Random. 1976. Old-fashioned pictures and large format make this an inviting collection. Rhymes on the same subject are clustered. (A)

Mother Goose: Seventy-seven Verses with Pictures, illus. by Tasha Tudor. Walck, 1944. Delicate pictures in pastel shades illustrate a small, easy-to-hold selection. (A)

Old Mother Hubbard and Her Dog, illus. by Evaline Ness. Holt, 1972. Paper, Holt/Owlet. Comical illustrations follow Mother Hubbard through a long day filled with attempts to please her old sheep-dog. (A-B)

Randolph Caldecott's John Gilpin and Other Stories. Warne, 1978. Four rhymes illustrated, line by line, by a master artist of the nine-teenth century. A long-time favorite. (A-B)

The Real Mother Goose, illus. by Blanche Fisher Wright. Rand, 1916. Simple, uncluttered illustrations in flat, bright colors have made this large and ample collection a long-time favorite. (A)

Rimes de la Mère Oie: Mother Goose Rhymes Rendered into French, ed. by Ormonde de Kay, Jr.; illus. by Seymour Chwast, Milton Glaser, and Barry Zaid. Little, 1971. If the French words are different, the rhythm remains the same. A beautiful, tall book with black-and-white silhouettes and designs interspersed among contemporary full-color spreads.. (A-B)

The Rooster Crows: A Book of American Rhymes and Jingles, illus. by Maud and Miska Petersham. Macmillan, 1945. Paper (abr. ed.), Collier/Macmillan.   This sprightly illustrated collection contains a few Old World rhymes together with many which are particularly American, such as "A bear went over the mountain."   (A-B)

Three Jovial Huntsmen: A Mother Goose Rhyme, ad. and illus. by Susan Jeffers. Bradbury, 1973. Paper, Penguin/Puffin.   Imaginative, delicately detailed illustrations show the adventures of foolish hunters who can't see the animals for the trees.   (A)

A B C Books

A B C Book, illus. by C. B. Falls. Doubleday, 1923. Paper, Doubleday.   Bold, poster-like woodcuts show a bird, beast, or fish for each letter of the alphabet.   (A)

The A B C Bunny, written and illus. by Wanda Gág. Coward, 1933. Paper, Coward.   A lively rabbit is the main character in this alphabet rhyme. You can say it as you turn the pages, and then sing it to the music on the last page.   (A)

Albert B. Cub & Zebra: An Alphabet Storybook, written and illus. by Anne Rockwell. Crowell, 1977.   Because Albert has lost Zebra, he looks for his friend throughout the whole book, searching from A to Z among the colorful and busy scenes.   (A-B)

Alphabet World, by Barry Miller. Macmillan, 1971.   Letters can be found everywhere, indoors and out, as these black-and-white photographs overlaid with letters on translucent paper show.   (A-B)

Anno's Alphabet: An Adventure in Imagination, by Mitsumasa Anno. Crowell, 1975.   Letters are shown as pieces of roughly grained wood, standing for intriguing objects that play tricks with the eyes of the readers.   (A-B)

Brian Wildsmith's A B C, Watts, 1963.   Stunning, colorful drawings illustrate the letters from apple to zebra, with each word printed in upper and lower case.   (A)

Bruno Munari's A B C. Philomel, 1960.   A clearly drawn and colorfully illustrated book which includes some whimsical touches by the artist.   (★A)

Handtalk: An A B C of Finger Spelling and Sign Language, by Remy Charlip and Mary Beth and George Ancona. Parents, 1974.   The alphabet of the deaf people is brought to life by involving readers with a gamelike approach.   (B-C)

Hosie's Alphabet, words by Hosea, Tobias, and Lisa Baskin; illus. by Leonard Baskin. Viking, 1972.   A sophisticated A B C which uses difficult words and stunning illustrations executed in a variety of techniques.   (A-C)

Jambo Means Hello: Swahili Alphabet Book, by Muriel Feelings; illus. by Tom Feelings. Dial, 1974.   A vivid impression of East African life is given, as well as words and their definitions representing each of the twenty-four letters in the Swahili alphabet. (B-C)

Teddybears A B C, by Susanna Gretz. Follett, 1975.   Five humorous bears go through the letters of the alphabet in their rather human everyday activities.   (A)

Counting Books

Billions of Bugs, written and illus. by Haris Petie. Prentice, 1975. The text moves from "1 praying mantis eating a grub" to "10 walking sticks hide in a shrub," and so on to 1,000 butterflies. (A-B)

Count and See, by Tana Hoban. Macmillan, 1972. Paper, Collier/Macmillan.   Photographs of objects familiar to a young child include numbers up to 100 peas in 10 pea pods.   (A)

Dancing in the Moon: Counting Rhymes, written and illus. by Fritz Eichenberg. Harcourt, 1956. Paper, Harcourt/Voyager. Animal antics and delightful nonsense rhymes accompany each number from one to twenty. (A)

Numbers, by John Reiss. Bradbury, 1971. Rich, bright colors illuminate familiar objects and large, clear numbers which go from 1 to 10, then by 10s to 100, and finally to 1,000 raindrops falling on an umbrella. (A-B)

Numbers of Things, by Helen Oxenbury. Watts. 1968. A tall, narrow book with deft, humorous illustrations introducing numbers 1 to 50. The final page shows an astronaut on the moon and asks: "How many stars?" (A-B)

One Dancing Drum: A Counting Book for Children (and Parents) Who Are Tired of Puppies, Chickens, and Horses, by Gail Kredenser; illus. by Stanley Mack. Phillips, 1971. A whimsical gathering of a group of instruments turns out to be a bit too large for the bandstand. (A-B)

One Old Oxford Ox, illus. by Nicola Bayley. Atheneum, 1977. Twelve counting rhymes, alliteratively patterned into imaginative and nonsensical verses, are also sophisticated tongue twisters. (B)

Thirteen, by Remy Charlip and Jerry Joyner. Parents, 1975. You can look through this book at least thirteen times and see different things, because there are thirteen different happenings simultaneously developing from page to page. (B)

The Very Hungry Caterpillar, by Eric Carle. Philomel, 1969. This colorful book counts the things eaten by the caterpillar during the week as it grows and changes into a beautiful butterfly. *1 2,3 to the Zoo* (Philomel, 1968) is another counting book by this illustrator. (★A)

Wordless Picture Books

The Adventures of Paddy Pork, written and illus. by John S. Goodall. Harcourt, 1968.   A young pig runs away from his mother to follow a small traveling circus. His adventures are depicted in detailed black-and-white drawings and half-page "what-will-happen-next?" inserts.   (A-B)

Apples, illus. by Nonny Hogrogian. Macmillan, 1972.   An apple orchard grows magically as people and animals carelessly scatter their apple cores.   (A-B)

The Bear and the Fly, illus. by Paula Winter. Crown, 1976.   The bear tries to swat a fly over and over again till his efforts result in disaster.   (A-B)

Bobo's Dream, illus. by Martha Alexander. Dial, 1970. Paper, Dial/Pied Piper.   Bobo, a grateful dachshund whose bone is rescued by his master, dreams of a heroic rescue in which he returns the favor. *Out, Out, Out* (Dial, 1968) is another wordless book by the same illustrator.   (A)

A Boy, a Dog, and a Frog, illus. by Mercer Mayer. Dial, 1967. Paper, Dial/Pied Piper.   On a summer day, a boy sets forth with his dog and a net to catch an enterprising and personable frog.   (A)

Brian Wildsmith's Circus, Watts, 1970.   Colorful pictures show the circus from a small boy's point of view.   (A-B)

Changes, Changes, illus. by Pat Hutchins. Macmillan, 1971. Paper, Collier/Macmillan.   Wooden dolls arrange and rearrange wooden building blocks to accommodate the needs of their eventful lives. (A-B)

Deep in the Forest, illus. by Brinton Turkle. Dutton, 1976.   The traditional story of "The Three Bears" is turned around as a bear decides to visit the home of some people who are out walking in the woods.   (A-B)

Do You Want to Be My Friend? illus. by Eric Carle. Crowell, 1971.   A mouse seeking a friend follows the lead of one tail after another, only to be surprised at what he finds.   (A-B)

The Good Bird, illus. by Peter Wezel. Harper, 1964.   In simple, crayoned pictures, a friendly pink bird shares its worm with an unhappy goldfish.   (A-B)

Look Again! illus. by Tana Hoban. Macmillan, 1971. Paper, Windmill.   A book of photographs in black and white invites the reader to look through a cut-out square at a portion of something larger. Sometimes it is difficult to guess what it is until you turn the page. *Shapes and Things* (Macmillan, 1970) is also composed of black-and-white photographs depicting things we use and see every day.   (A-B)

Look What I Can Do, illus. by Jose Aruego. Scribner, 1971. Paper, Scribner.   Two brown-and-gray carabaos match each other's antics in a game of follow-the-leader, until a third carabao challenges them.   (B)

Sebastian and the Mushroom, illus. by Fernando Krahn. Delacorte, 1976.   In detailed line drawings a small boy discovers that the mushroom's possibilities are unlimited, that it can take him to the stars. *The Self-Made Snowman* (Lippincott, 1974) is another of Krahn's creative wordless stories.   (B)

Snail, Where Are You? illus. by Tomi Ungerer. Harper, 1962.   On every page is a brightly colored picture in which, if you look hard enough, you can find a snail.   (A-B)

Topsy-Turvies: Pictures to Stretch the Imagination, illus. by Mitsumasa Anno. Weatherhill, 1970.   Droll scenes and characters that portray things which are different upside down than right side up.   (A-B)

Picture Story Books

Anatole and the Cat, by Eve Titus and illus. by Paul Galdone. McGraw, 1956.   Anatole, an "anonymouse" cheese taster in a factory, is the most contented mouse in "All of France." There are several other books about him, his family, and his friends. (B)

Andy and the Lion, written and illus. by James Daugherty. Viking, 1938. Paper, Penguin/Puffin. Andy, who likes to read about lions, meets one on his way to school. After Andy pulls a thorn from the lion's paw they become friends for life. A picture-book variant of "Androcles and the Lion." (A-B)

Ask Mr. Bear, written and illus. by Marjorie Flack. Macmillan, 1932. Paper, Collier/Macmillan. A small boy with the help of the farm animals tries to find just the right birthday present for his mother. (★A)

The Biggest Bear, written and illus. by Lynd Ward. Houghton, 1952. Paper, Houghton/Sandpiper. Johnny brings home a bear cub as a pet; but as the cub grows, so do Johnny's problems. (A-B)

Blueberries for Sal, written and illus. by Robert McCloskey. Viking, 1948. Paper, Penguin/Puffin. Blue-and-white pictures portray Sal and her mother gathering blueberries on the same mountain as little bear and his mother. *One Morning in Maine* (Viking, 1952. Paper, Penguin/Puffin) continues the story of Sal and her family on the day she loses her first tooth. (A)

The Box with Red Wheels, written and illus. by Maud and Miska Petersham. Macmillan, 1949. Paper, Collier/Macmillan. One by one, animals come into the yard to peer at the baby who sleeps in the box with the red wheels. (★A)

Buzz, Buzz, Buzz, written and illus. by Byron Barton. Macmillan, 1973. Paper, Penguin/Puffin. When a bee stings a bull, a great chain of lively events begins. (A-B)

The Camel Who Took a Walk, by Jack Tworkov; illus. by Roger Duvoisin. Dutton, 1951. Paper, Dutton/Anytime. Just as a gentle, unsuspecting camel gets to the place where the tiger plans to pounce on her, she stops and says, "I think I'll go back." (A-B)

Caps for Sale, written and illus. by Esphyr Slobodkina. Addison-Wesley, 1947. Paper, Scholastic/Starline. While a tired pedlar sleeps, some mischievous monkeys take all the caps he has piled on his head. (★A)

Chanticleer and the Fox, by Geoffrey Chaucer; illus. by Barbara Cooney. Crowell, 1958.   "The Nun's Tale" of the wily fox, who almost flatters the vain cock into becoming his dinner, is given authentic and lively pictures in bright colors.   (B)

The Church Mouse, written and illus. by Graham Oakley. Atheneum, 1972. Paper, Atheneum/Aladdin.   Arthur and his many mouse associates live and work in the same British church with Samson the cat who is usually, but not always, meek and pious. This is the first of several church mouse stories.   (A-B)

Corduroy, written and illus. by Don Freeman. Viking, 1968. Paper, Penguin/Puffin.   An engaging teddy bear, unsold in a department store because one of his overall buttons is missing, has an exciting nighttime adventure and finds the home he has always wanted.   (A-B)

Crow Boy, written and illus. by Taro Yashima. Viking, 1955. Paper, Penguin/Puffin.   A shy, lonely, sensitive Japanese boy is finally recognized by his classmates through his teacher's understanding and encouragement.   (A-B)

Curious George, written and illus. by Hans A. Rey. Houghton, 1941. Paper, Houghton/Sandpiper.   Curiosity causes the capture of a small jungle monkey and continues to bring him exciting adventures on his boat trip to America. This is the first of several stories about George.   (A-B)

Drummer Hoff, ad. by Barbara Emberley; illus. by Ed Emberley. Prentice, 1967. Paper, Prentice.   Brightly colored woodcuts illustrate this lively cumulative rhyme in which various soldiers brought parts of the cannon, but "Drummer Hoff fired it off."   (A-B)

Evan's Corner, by Elizabeth Starr Hill. Holt, 1967. Paper, Holt/ Owlet.   A small boy finds there is satisfaction in having a corner of his own, but that pleasure is increased by sharing it with a younger brother. A story of urban life.   (B)

Find the Cat, by Elaine Livermore. Houghton, 1973. Paper, Houghton. A dog is looking for the cat in this simple story with complicated pictures. A reader trying to find the cat in the pictures is sometimes as mystified as the dog.   (A-B)

Fish for Supper, by M. B. Goffstein. Dial, 1976. Droll line drawings and a spare text describe grandmother's day as she catches fish and then carefully cooks them for her solitary supper. (A-B)

Garth Pig and the Ice-Cream Lady, by Mary Rayner. Atheneum, 1977. When Garth Pig is chosen by his nine brothers and sisters to buy ice cream for all of them, he discovers—almost too late—that the ice-cream lady is a wolf. (A-B)

Gilberto and the Wind, written and illus. by Marie Hall Ets. Viking, 1963. Paper, Penguin/Puffin. With pictures in which one can almost feel the wind blowing, a small Hispanic boy tells of his adventures on a windy day. (A-B)

Goodnight Moon, by Margaret Wise Brown; illus. by Clement Hurd. Harper, 1947. Paper, Harper/Trophy. A small rabbit says goodnight to a roomful of familiar objects which very young children will easily recognize. Rhythmic text and quiet pictures make this a good bedtime book. (★A)

Guess Who My Favorite Person Is? by Byrd Baylor; illus. by Robert Parker. Scribner, 1977.   The author meets a small girl in a field and they talk about their favorite things. (B)

The Happy Lion, by Louise Fatio; illus. by Roger Duvoisin. McGraw, 1954.   Everyone is friendly with the lion in the Parisian zoo until he escapes from his cage and tries to return their visits. The pictures have a lively French flavor. (A-B)

The Happy Owls, by Celestino Piatti. Atheneum, 1964. Paper, Atheneum/Aladdin.   All the animals consult the owls to discover the secret of happiness. (A-B)

Harry, the Dirty Dog, by Gene Zion; illus. by Margaret Bloy Graham. Harper, 1956. Paper, Harper/Trophy. The engaging Harry buries the scrub brush and spends a glorious day getting dirty; later he finds that soap has its uses after all. More stories about Harry's adventures are available. (A-B)

Hildilid's Night, by Cheli D. Ryan; illus. by Arnold Lobel. Macmillan, 1971. Paper, Collier/Macmillan. Hildilid hates the night and tries to chase it away by all sorts of methods. However, she does not succeed until the sun comes up and she is too tired to appreciate it. (A-B)

The House on East 88th Street, by Bernard Waber. Houghton, 1962. Paper, Houghton/Sandpiper. When the Primm family moves into its apartment at this address, they find Lyle, a performing crocodile, in the bathtub. There are several other books about Lyle. (B)

Inch by Inch, by Leo Lionni. Astor, 1960. An inchworm saves himself from a hungry robin by proving his usefulness as a measurer. The pictures are large and brightly colored. (A-B)

Johnny Crow's Garden: A Picture Book, drawn by L. Leslie Brooke. Warne, 1903. Paper, Watts. The fine humor of the drawings of the grand party of animals has made this book a favorite of several generations. (★A)

Little Bear, by Else H. Minarik; illus. by Maurice Sendak. Harper, 1957. Paper, Harper/Trophy. Four stories full of warmth, tenderness, and humor about an appealing bear cub that are easy to read and to hear. A number of other books about Little Bear, his family, and his friends are available. (A-B)

Little Tim and the Brave Sea Captain, written and illus. by Edward Ardizzone. Reprint of 1936 ed.; Oxford, 1978. A small British boy who loves boats becomes a stowaway and is shipwrecked. Look for additional sea stories about this precocious hero. (A-B)

Madeline, by Ludwig Bemelmans. Viking, 1939. Paper, Penguin/ Puffin. Detailed pictures and amusing rhymes create the atmosphere of Paris and introduce us to a charming nonconformist. Other picture stories describe further adventures of Madeline. (A-B)

Make Way for Ducklings, written and illus. by Robert McCloskey. Viking, 1941. Paper, Penguin/Puffin. Mrs. Mallard and her ducklings complicate Boston traffic when they move from the Charles River to a new home in Boston's Public Gardens. (A-B)

Martin's Father, 2nd ed., by Margrit Eichler; illus. by Bev Magennis. Lollipop Power, 1977. Paper, Lollipop Power. "Martin has the best father in the world." They would do laundry together, walk together, make sandwiches together, and ever so much more. (B)

May I Bring a Friend? by Beatrice Schenk de Regniers; illus. by Beni Montresor. Atheneum, 1964. Paper, Atheneum/Aladdin.   The king and queen enjoy all the animal friends that their guest brings to tea. (A-B)

Mike Mulligan and His Steam Shovel, written and illus. by Virginia Lee Burton. Houghton, 1939. Paper, Houghton/Sandpiper.   Mike and Mary Anne, his old steam shovel, dig themselves into a cellar and cannot get out. Another detailed, illustrated book by this author is *The Little House* (Houghton, 1942. Paper, Houghton/Sandpiper.) (A-B)

Millions of Cats, by Wanda Gág. Coward, 1928. Paper, Coward.   The very old man goes out to look for one little cat but comes home with many more. He and the very old woman can't decide which one to keep, but the cats settle that problem in their own way.   (A-B)

Mr. Gumpy's Outing, by John Burningham. Holt, 1971.   Mr. Gumpy admonishes each animal and child not to misbehave as he takes them into his boat; but they all do anyway, the boat tips over, and then they have tea!   (★A)

Mommy, Buy Me a China Doll, ad. by Harve Zemach; illus. by Margot Zemach. Reprint of 1966 ed., Farrar, 1975.   In this Ozark folk song, a small girl suggests a ridiculous swapping of sleeping places in order to justify having the china doll she wants so badly.   (★A-B)

Mouse Tales, by Arnold Lobel. Harper, 1972. Paper, Harper/Trophy. Papa mouse tells short bedtime tales for each of his seven mouse boys. Amply and lovingly illustrated.   (A-B)

Noah's Ark, ad. and illus. by Peter Spier. Doubleday, 1977.   The familiar Old Testament story is given a fresh new interpretation in watercolor illustrations that are full of humor and minute details, accompanied by a translation of a seventeenth-century Dutch poem.   (B)

Nothing Ever Happens on Our Block, by Ellen Raskin. Atheneum, 1966. Paper, Atheneum/Aladdin.   This is what bored Chester says as he sits on the curb; however, anyone who studies the pictures will find some amazing happenings going on behind Chester. (A-B)

One Monday Morning, written and illus. by Uri Shulevitz. Scribner, 1967. Paper, Scribner. Each day in the week a small boy in a New York apartment makes believe that a king and his retinue are coming to visit. *Rain Rain Rivers* (Farrar, 1969), also by Shulevitz, depicts the mood of a rainy day in story and in watercolor illustrations. (A-B)

Pelle's New Suit, by Else Beskow. Harper, 1929. Paper, Scholastic. In a story translated from the Swedish, the making of Pelle's suit is described from lamb to tailor. Large, realistic illustrations depict the Sweden of yesterday. (A-B)

Pierre: A Cautionary Tale in Five Chapters and a Prologue, by Maurice Sendak. Harper, 1962. This, the story of a boy who learned to care, is one of four volumes in the *Nutshell Library* (Harper, 1962). (A-B)

A Pocketful of Cricket, by Rebecca Caudill, illus. by Evaline Ness. Holt, 1964. Paper, Holt/Owlet. When Jay takes his cricket with him on the first day of school, an understanding teacher accepts it as a bridge between home and the classroom. (A-B)

Play with Me, written and illus. by Marie Hall Ets. Viking, 1955. Paper, Penguin/Puffin. A small girl finally finds a playmate among the meadow creatures when she learns not to run after them. *In the Forest* (Viking, 1944. Paper, Penguin/Puffin), also by Ets, describes an imaginative party a small boy has with his animal friends. (★A)

Rosie's Walk, by Pat Hutchins. Macmillan, 1968. Paper, Collier/ Macmillan. Rosie, a determined, flatfooted hen, goes for a walk unmindful of the fact that she is being stalked by a hungry fox. Another droll story by Hutchins is *The Surprise Party* (Macmillan, 1969. Paper, Collier/Macmillan). (A-B)

Sam, by Anne H. Scott; illus. by Symeon Shimin. McGraw, 1967. Everyone in Sam's family shoos him away, not understanding until later the cumulative effect on the smallest member. (A-B)

The Shrinking of Treehorn, by Florence Parry Heide, with drawings by Edward Gorey. Holiday, 1971. Paper, Dell. Treehorn, an already small boy, begins to shrink. He tries to point this out to his teacher and his parents, but at first they don't notice, and then they don't think it is appropriate behavior. (B)

The Snowy Day, written and illus. by Ezra Jack Keats. Viking, 1962. Paper, Penguin/Puffin.   Footprints in the snow mark small Peter's travels during a wonderful, fun-filled day outdoors.   (A-B)

The Story about Ping, by Marjorie Flack; illus. by Kurt Wiese. Viking, 1933. Paper, Penguin/Puffin.   A small duck who lives on a wise-eyed boat on the Yangtze River encounters numerous adventures when he tries to avoid a spanking.   (A-B)

The Story of Babar, the Little Elephant, by Jean de Brunhoff. Random, 1933.   A young elephant leaves the jungle to live in Paris. When he returns home, he is proclaimed king of the elephants. Colorful and detailed illustrations portray Babar's eventful tale. And there are more Babar stories after this!   (A-B)

The Story of Ferdinand, by Munro Leaf; illus. by Robert Lawson. Viking, 1936. Paper, Penguin/Puffin.   This bull doesn't really want to fight; he prefers to smell the flowers while sitting quietly under his favorite tree.   (A-B)

The Tale of Peter Rabbit, written and illus. by Beatrix Potter. Warne, 1902. Paper, Dover.   A small book contains the perennial favorite story of Peter and his misadventures in Mr. McGregor's garden. One of many animal stories in the same format by Potter.   (A-B)

Time of Wonder, by Robert McCloskey. Viking, 1957. Paper, Penguin/Puffin.   Poetic words and pastel watercolors tell of a late summer storm on an island in Maine.   (A-B)

The Tomten, ad. by Astrid Lindgren from a poem by Viktor Rydberg; illus. by Harald Wiberg. Coward, 1961. Paper, Coward.   A protecting troll watches over a Swedish farm and its animals in the quiet dark of winter. The accompanying watercolors are as dark, quiet, and magical as the story.   (B)

Umbrella. written and illus. by Taro Yashima. Viking, 1958. Paper, Penguin/Puffin.   A small Japanese-American girl has to wait a very long time before she can use her new umbrella.   (A)

What Do You Say, Dear? by Sesyle Joslin, pictures by Maurice Sendak. Addison, 1958. Paper, Scholastic.   Exaggerated humor marks this question-and-answer book, which is also an introduction to manners.   (A-B)

Where the Wild Things Are, written and illus. by Maurice Sendak. Harper, 1963.   Max, who is naughty, is sent to bed without supper, and off he goes to the land of the wild things. There he becomes king of the fierce and comical creatures and has a wild rumpus with them until he decides to go home.   (A-B)

White Snow, Bright Snow, by Alvin Tresselt; illus. by Roger Duvoisin. Lothrop, 1947.   The happenings in a small town during a snowy winter, from the first flake to the first crocus of spring. Other poetical books by Tresselt about the weather include *Hide and Seek Fog* (Lothrop, 1965) and *Rain Drop Splash* (Lothrop, 1946).   (A-B)

Who Owns the Moon? by Sonia Levitin; illus. by John Larrecq. Parnassus, 1973.   Three farmers who are always arguing finally find an agreeable answer to this difficult question.   (B)

Whose Mouse Are You? by Robert Kraus; pictures by Jose Aruego. Macmillan, 1970. Paper, Collier/Macmillan.   A little mouse, bereft of his family, determinedly finds them again. Vivid pictures in flamboyant color complement the text.   (★A)

William's Doll, by Charlotte Zolotow; illus. by William Pène du Bois. Harper, 1972.   William is teased because he wants a doll; only his grandmother understands that both boys and girls can enjoy playing at being a parent.   (A-B)

The Winter Bear, by Ruth Craft; illus. by Erik Blegvad. A Margaret K. McElderry Book/Atheneum, 1975.   Paper, Atheneum/Aladdin. Full-color pictures capture the beauty of this unusual bear's surroundings.   (A)

Folk- and Fairy Tales

Picture Book Editions

The Angry Moon, ret. by William Sleator; pictures by Blair Lent. Atlantic-Little, 1970. The moon kidnaps an Indian girl who laughs at him. Imaginative paintings based on Tlingit motifs complement the text. (B)

Arrow to the Sun: A Pueblo Indian Tale, ad. and illus. by Gerald McDermott. Viking, 1974. Paper, Penguin/Puffin. How the boy found his father, the Lord of the Sun, is dramatically illustrated in brilliant colors and striking designs. (B-C)

Cinderella, by Charles Perrault; illus. by Marcia Brown. Scribner, 1954. Paper, Scribner. The beloved favorite of so many children is softly interpreted in pinks and blues. (A-B)

Cricket Boy: A Chinese Tale, ret. by Feenie Ziner; illus. by Ed Young. Doubleday, 1977. A tiny cricket fights the Emperor's champion in this haunting tale of honor and transformation. (B-C)

Crickets and Frogs: A Fable in Spanish and English. by Gabriela Mistral; illus. by Antonio Frasconi. A Margaret K. McElderry Book/ Atheneum, 1972. Translated and adapted by Doris Dana, this fable tells of the cacaphony created when the crickets and the frogs try to compete with each other in song. (B-C)

The Cuckoo's Reward/El Premio del Cuco: A Folk Tale from Mexico in Spanish and English, ad. and tr. by Daisy Kouzel; illus. by Earl Thollander. Doubleday, 1977. A traditional Mexican tale reveals how the cuckoo lost her beautiful feathers and why she lays her eggs in other birds' nests. (B-C)

The Emperor and the Kite, by Jane Yolen; illus. by Ed Young. World, 1967. The story of the daughter of a Chinese emperor who rescued her imprisoned father by flying him a kite made of her own hair. Exquisitely illustrated in color with paper cuttings. (B-C)

The Fool of the World and the Flying Ship: A Russian Tale, ret. by Arthur Ransome; illus. by Uri Shulevitz. Farrar, 1968. A lively story from *Old Peter's Russian Tales,* retold with colorful panoramic illustrations. (B)

How Djadja-Em-Ankh Saved the Day: A Tale from Ancient Egypt, with illus. and commentary by Lise Manniche. Crowell, 1977. A vignette from the Fifth Dynasty is used to introduce Egyptian life and hieroglyphs. Translated from the original Hieratic. (B-C)

It Could Always Be Worse: A Yiddish Folk Tale, ret. and illus. by Margot Zemach. Farrar, 1977. Paper, Scholastic. Colorful, humorous illustrations enhance an uproarious tale about a poor man and his family crowded into a one-room hut. (B)

Journey Cake, Ho! by Ruth Sawyer; illus. by Robert McCloskey. Viking, 1953. Paper, Penguin/Puffin. The old folktale about the runaway johnnycake is retold with rollicking illustrations. (A-B)

Little Red Hen, pictures by Janina Domanska. Macmillan, 1973. The little red hen did all the work and her friends got their just deserts. Humorous illustrations in a well-designed book. (A)

The Monkey and the Crocodile: A Jataka Tale from India, ret. and illus. by Paul Galdone. Seabury, 1969. Both text and pictures are full of humor in this tale of mischief and gullibility. (B)

My Mother Is the Most Beautiful Woman in the World: A Russian Folktale, ret. by Becky Reyher; illus. by Ruth Gannett. Lothrop, 1945. A small child, Varya, lost in the wheatfields of the Ukraine, can only describe her mother as "the most beautiful woman in the world." (A-B)

The Old Woman and Her Pig, illus. by Paul Galdone. McGraw, 1960. This familiar, repetitive nursery tale is delightfully illustrated in color and black and white. (A)

Once a Mouse . . . A Fable Cut in Wood, by Marcia Brown. Scribner, 1961. Once a mouse, always a mouse is the lesson of this Indian fable about a hermit who transforms a mouse into a tiger. (B)

The Pumpkin Giant, ret. by Ellin Greene from a version by Mary E. Wilkins; illus. by Trina Schart Hyman. Lothrop, 1970. In this tale reader and listener meet a princess so fat that she can only roll, not walk. (B-C)

Puss in Boots, ad. and illus. by Marcia Brown. Scribner, 1952. Perrault's beloved tale about the cat who helped his master win a fortune is happily illustrated in soft pastels.   (A-B)

The Rabbi and the Twenty-nine Witches: A Talmudic Legend, ret. and illus. by Marilyn Hirsh. Holiday, 1976. Paper, Scholastic.   The Rabbi's clever plan rids his village of the "meanest, scariest, ugliest, wickedest witches that ever were."   (B)

The Ring in the Prairie: A Shawnee Legend, ed. by John Bierhorst; with pictures by Leo and Diane Dillon. Dial, 1970. Paper, Dial/Pied Piper.   An Indian brave falls in love with a spirit maiden. Dramatic, colorful drawings express the story's poetic quality.   (B)

The Shoemaker and the Elves, by J. L. K. Grimm and W. K. Grimm; illus. by Adrienne Adams. Scribner, 1960. Paper, Scribner.   Elves help a poor shoemaker who, in turn, rewards them with new clothes. Sprightly watercolor illustrations.   (A-B)

The Sleeping Beauty, ret. and illus. by Trina Schart Hyman. Little, 1977.   The beloved story is retold with romantic and warmly human illustrations. *Snow White* (Little, 1975. Paper, Little), in a translation by Paul Heins, has romantic illustrations by this same artist.   (A-C)

Strega Nona: An Old Tale, ret. and illus. by Tomie de Paola. Prentice, 1975.   Strega Nona's magic pasta pot fed and filled the town because Big Anthony did not know how to stop it.   (A-B)

The Three Bears, ed. and illus. by Paul Galdone. Seabury, 1972. Paper, Scholastic.   A humorously illustrated version of one of the best-known of all folktales.   (★A)

The Three Billy Goats Gruff, by P. C. Asbjørnsen and J. E. Moe; illus. by Marcia Brown. Harcourt, 1957. Paper, Harcourt/Voyager.   The simple tale of the troll who meets his match in Big Billy Goat Gruff is dramatically enlivened by the colorful illustrations. (★A)

The Three Poor Tailors, ret. and illus. by Victor G. Ambrus. Harcourt, 1966.   Ambrus retells an old folktale from his native Hungary and enlivens it with rollicking pictures in glowing colors.   (B)

Three Strong Women: A Tall Tale from Japan, by Claus Stamm; illus. by Kazue Mizumura. Viking, 1962. Paper, Penguin/Puffin.   A young wrestler improves his art with the help of three peasant women.   (B)

Tom Tit Tot: An English Folk Tale, illus. by Evaline Ness. Scribner, 1965.   A variant of "Rumpelstiltskin," this vigorous folktale is illustrated with handsome woodcuts.   (A-B)

The Wave, by Margaret Hodges; illus. by Blair Lent. Houghton, 1964. To save his village from a tidal wave, an old man sacrifices his wealth and sets fire to his rice fields on the mountain. A handsomely illustrated retelling of Lafcadio Hearn's *Gleanings in Buddha-fields.*   (B-C)

Why Mosquitoes Buzz in People's Ears: A West African Tale, ret. by Verna Aardema; pictures by Leo and Diane Dillon. Dial, 1975. Paper, Dial/Pied Piper.   The trouble began when mosquito told lies so big that iguana put sticks in his ears to stop the sound. (A-B)

Why the Sun and the Moon Live in the Sky: An African Folktale, by Elphinstone Dayrell; illus. by Blair Lent. Houghton, 1968. Paper, Houghton/Sandpiper.   An attractive version of an old and interesting myth.   (A-B)

Wild Robin, ret. and illus. by Susan Jeffers. Dutton, 1976.   Sister Janet saves young Robin from the Queen of Fairyland in this beautifully illustrated variant of the Tamlane legend.   (B)

Collections

Anansi the Spider Man, by Philip Sherlock; illus. by Marcia Brown. Crowell, 1954.   Jamaican folktales about Br'er Anansi, sometimes a man and sometimes a spider.   (B-C)

The Arabian Nights: Tales of Wonder and Magnificance, sel. and ed. by Padraic Colum; illus. by Lynd Ward. Macmillan, 1953.   There

are nine stories in this distinctive edition of a favorite classic.
(B-C)

Baba Yaga's Geese and Other Russian Stories, tr. and ad. by Bonnie
Carey; illus. by Guy Fleming. Indiana, 1973. Paper, Indiana.
A lively assortment of popular tales from the oral tradition, attrac-
tively designed and illustrated.   (B-C)

The Beggar in the Blanket and Other Vietnamese Tales, ret. by Gail B.
Graham; illus. by Brigitte Bryan. Dial, 1970.   The exotic flavor of
the East permeates this collection drawn from French-language
sources.   (B-C)

Clever Cooks, comp. by Ellin Greene; illus. by Trina Schart Hyman.
Lothrop, 1973. Paper, Scholastic.   "A concoction of stories,
charms, recipes, and riddles" that will delight children.   (B-C)

East of the Sun and West of the Moon and Other Tales, col. by P. C.
Asbjørnsen and J. E. Moe; illus. by Tom Vroman. Macmillan,
1963.   Among these twelve well-known Norwegian folktales are
"Princess on the Glass Hill," and "The Giant Who Had No Heart in
His Body."   (B-C)

The Fables of Aesop, sel. by Joseph Jacobs; illus. by David Levine.
Macmillan, 1964.   The illustrations in this edition create new
interest in over eighty fables selected for young readers.   (B-C)

Favorite Fairy Tales Told in Denmark, ret. by Virginia Haviland; illus.
by Margot Zemach. Little, 1971.   A lively selection with appeal for
young readers. Another attractive collection in this series is *Favorite Fairy Tales Told in Greece,* illus. by Nonny Hogrogian (Little,
1970).   (B)

Greedy Mariani and Other Folktales of the Antilles, sel. and ad. by
Dorothy S. Carter; illus. by Trina Schart Hyman. A Margaret K.
McElderry Book/Atheneum, 1974.   Caribbean tales of tricksters,
animals, and magic.   (B-C)

The Hat-shaking Dance and Other Tales from Ghana, by Harold Cour-
lander with Albert K. Prempeh; illus. by Enrico Arno. Harcourt,
1957.   These wise and humorous folktales from the Ashanti people of Africa include many about Anansi, the spider. Fun to read
and wonderful to tell.   (B-C)

Heather and Broom: Tales of the Scottish Highlands, ed. by Sorche Nic Leodhas; illus. by Consuelo Joerns. Holt, 1960.   A collection of readable and tellable tales that could only take place in Scotland. Another collection of tales and legends by this author is *Thistle and Thyme,* illus. by Evaline Ness (Holt, 1962).   (B-C)

The Jack Tales, ed. by Richard Chase; illus. by Berkeley Williams, Jr. Houghton, 1943.   Jack conquers giants, dragons, and kings in authentic Appalachian folk style. Good fun to read and tell. A similar collection is *Grandfather Tales* (Houghton, 1948).   (B-C)

Jataka Tales, ed. by Nancy DeRoin; original drawings by Ellen Lanyon. Houghton, 1975. Paper, Dell.   Forty retellings of the Buddha's fables dealing with such human frailties as greed, fear, and talkativeness.   (B-C)

Just So Stories (Anniversary ed.), by Rudyard Kipling; illus. by Etienne Delessert. Doubleday, 1972.   The original text with arresting modern illustrations.   (B-C)

The Knee-High Man and Other Tales, by Julius Lester; pictures by Ralph Pinto. Dial, 1972.   Simple retellings of animal tales from the stories originally told by slaves.   (B)

Let's Steal the Moon: Jewish Tales, Ancient and Recent, ret. by Blanche L. Serwer; illus. by Trina Schart Hyman. Little, 1970."Witches' tales, tall tales, and foolish tales, all full of the wisdom and humor so much a part of the Jewish culture."   (B)

The Magic Orange Tree and Other Haitian Folktales, col. by Diane Wolkstein; illus. by Elsa Henriquez. Knopf, 1978.   A storyteller shares her pleasure in the art and conveys a vivid sense of the way it thrives in modern Haiti.   (C-D)

The Mouse Woman and the Mischief-Makers, by Christie Harris; drawings by Douglas Tait. Atheneum, 1977.   A collection of folktales from the Northwest Coast Indians in which Mouse Woman deals neatly with greedy humans, spirit creatures, and other beings.   (C-D)

Rootabaga Stories, by Carl Sandburg. Harcourt, 1951. Paper, Harcourt/ Voyager.   One of America's great writers relates in strong, poetic prose a number of stories filled with humor and strange persons.   (C-D)

Seven Tales, by Hans Christian Andersen; tr. by Eva Le Gallienne; pictures by Maurice Sendak. Harper, 1959. "The Ugly Duckling," "The Fir Tree," and other favorites are included in this collection. (B-C)

Tales from Grimm, freely tr. and illus. by Wanda Gág. Coward, 1936. A selection of some of the most suitable "Household Stories," translated with zest and humor for the younger child, with drawings that capture their peasant flavor. *More Tales from Grimm* (Coward, 1947) is also delightful. (A-B)

Tales from Silver Lands, by Charles J. Finger; illus. by Paul Honoré. Doubleday, 1925. A distinguished retelling of legends of the South American Indians, excellent for reading aloud. (C-D)

The Talking Cat and Other Stories of French Canada, by Natalie Savage Carlson; illus. by Roger Duvoisin. Harper, 1952. Spirited, witty folktales collected by an author who knows French Canada and its people. Lively black-and-white illustrations. (B-C)

The Three Bears and 15 Other Stories, sel. and illus. by Anne Rockwell. Crowell, 1975. Favorite versions of such best-loved nursery tales as "The Gingerbread Boy," "The Three Little Pigs," and "Little Red Riding Hood" in an attractive and profusely illustrated volume. (★A-B)

Womenfolk and Fairy Tales, ed. by Rosemary Minard; illus. by Suzanna Klein. Houghton, 1975. A lively collection of tales in which women prevail. An introduction to the volume provides a defense of fairy tales for those concerned about role stereotypes. (B-D)

The Wonder Clock, written and illus. by Howard Pyle. Harper, 1915. Paper, Dover. "Four and twenty marvelous tales being one for each hour of the day"; old folktales and legends retold. (B-D)

Zlateh the Goat and Other Stories, by Isaac Bashevis Singer; tr. from the Yiddish by the author and Elizabeth Shub; illus. by Maurice Sendak. Harper, 1966. This collection of seven Old World stories with an earthy and unique beauty will charm and amuse the story-teller and the listener, young and old. (B-C)

Tall Tales, Myths
and Legends

The Story of King Arthur and His Knights, by Howard Pyle, Scribner, 1903. Paper, Dover. The King Arthur stories for young people. (C-D)

The Children's Homer: The Adventures of Odysseus and the Tale of Troy, ed. by Padraic Colum; illus. by Willy Pogany. Macmillan, 1918. This satisfying retelling of "The Iliad" and "The Odyssey" has black-and-white drawings which are in keeping with classical tradition. (C-D)

d'Aulaires' Book of Greek Myths, ret. and illus. by Ingri and Edgar Parin d'Aulaire. Doubleday, 1962. Paper, Doubleday/Zephyr. The myths of Zeus, Hermes, Athena, Persephone, and Orpheus are retold in fresh, rhythmic prose. Handsome illustrations, glowing in color, match the strength and vigor of the tales. *Norse Gods and Giants* (Doubleday, 1967), also by the d'Aulaires, is a similar book of Norse myths. Their *Trolls* (Doubleday, 1972. Paper, Doubleday/Zephyr) describes the various kinds of trolls found in Norway and relates some of the stories associated with them. (B-C)

Hero Tales from Many Lands, comp. by Alice I. Hazeltine; illus. by Gordon Laite. Abingdon, 1961. This excellent collection includes thirty fragments of heroic literature, ranging from Japan to America, that provide enjoyable reading and listening as well as a valuable introduction to epic literature. (C-D)

The Impossible People: A History Natural and Unnatural of Beings Terrible and Wonderful, by Georgess McHargue; illus. by Frank Bozzo. Holt, 1972. Paper, Dell/Yearling. For the child who is curious about monsters and interested in their origins. (B-C)

John Henry: An American Legend, written and illus. by Ezra Jack Keats. Pantheon, 1965. Keats vividly retells the story of the American folk hero renowned for his feats as a railroad builder. Bold, dramatic woodcut illustrations are an integral part of this picture-book version. (A-B)

The Merry Adventures of Robin Hood, written and illus. by Howard Pyle. Scribner, 1946. Paper, Dover. Of all versions of the Robin Hood stories, this is the best loved. *Some Merry Adventures of Robin Hood* (rev. ed., Scribner, 1954) by the same author is for younger children. (B-C)

Ol' Paul: The Mighty Logger, written and illus. by Glen Rounds. Holiday, 1949. Paper, Avon/Camelot. The subtitle states that this is "a true account of the seemingly incredible exploits and inventions of the great Paul Bunyan, profusely illustrated by drawings made at the scene by the author. . . ." (B-C)

Pecos Bill: The Greatest Cowboy of All Time, by James C. Bowman; illus. by Laura Bannon. Whitman, 1937. Here is a cowboy who can do anything—well, almost anything! (B-D)

Rip Van Winkle and the Legend of Sleepy Hollow, by Washington Irving; illus. by David Levine. Macmillan, 1963. Lively pictures enhance these two famous short stories set in the Catskill Mountains.

Stories of the Gods and Heroes, by Sally Benson; illus. by Steele Savage. Dial, 1940. Paper, Dell. An interesting and easy-to-read version of the tales of the Trojan War, based on Bulfinch's *Age of Fable.* (B-C)

Thunder of the Gods, by Dorothy Hosford; illus. by Claire and George Loudon. Holt, 1952. Legends of the Norse gods are related simply and concisely. Included are stories about Odin, Thor, Balder, and Loki. (C-D)

Sing-Aloud Books

"Lap" Singing

The Foolish Frog, by Pete and Charles Seeger; illus. by Miloslav Jagr. Macmillan, 1973. This folk song about a singing farmer and a foolish frog was sung to Pete Seeger when he was five by his father. The music is adapted from an old song.   (A-B)

The Fox Went Out on a Chilly Night: An Old Song, illus. by Peter Spier. Doubleday, 1961. Paper, Doubleday.   On a moonlit night the fox goes foraging in a New England village to find supper for his family. Colorful, detailed drawings make this old song a new delight. *The Erie Canal* (Doubleday, 1970. Paper, Doubleday) is another old American folk song Peter Spier has illustrated.   (A-B)

Frog Went A-Courtin', ret. by John Langstaff; illus. by Feodor Rojankovsky. Harcourt, 1955. Paper, Harcourt/Voyager.   A happy combination of several versions of the old ballad about the wedding of the frog and the mouse.   (★A-B)

Go Tell Aunt Rhody, illus. by Aliki. Macmillan, 1975.   Lines from the old folk song accompany the illustrations in this richly colored picture book with a primitive American flavor.   (A-B)

Hush, Little Baby, by Margot Zemach. Dutton, 1976.   A familiar lullaby with illustrations showing the family in a Victorian setting.   (A)

One Wide River to Cross, ad. by Barbara Emberley; illus. by Ed Emberley. Prentice, 1966.   The animals of Noah's ark troop through the pages of an amusing version of the spiritual illustrated with woodcuts.   (A)

Over in the Meadow, by John Langstaff; illus. by Feodor Rojankovsky. Harcourt, 1957. Paper, Harcourt/Voyager.   The animals of the meadow are the subjects of this lilting, brightly colored, counting rhyme.   (★A)

Pop! Goes the Weasel and Yankee Doodle, illus. by Robert Quackenbush. Lippincott, 1976.   Includes the words of both songs, a map and tour guide of 1776 Manhattan, together with spritely illustrations. Two other song picture books by this illustrator are *Clementine* (Lippincott, 1974), and *Skip to My Lou* (Lippincott, 1975). (A-B)

Six Little Ducks, ret. and illus. by Chris Conover. Crowell, 1976.   The heroes of the old camp song are presented in a contemporary setting in this wittily illustrated book.   (A)

Collections for
Singing and Playing

American Folk Songs for Children in Home, School and Nursery School: A Book for Children, Parents and Teachers, by Ruth Porter Seeger; illus. by Barbara Cooney. Doubleday, 1948. Paper, Doubleday/Zephyr.   A long-time favorite volume which also provides directions for improvisations and rhythmic or dramatic play. (A-D)

A Fiesta of Folk Songs of Spain and Latin America, ed. by Henrietta Yurchenco; illus. by Jules Maidoff. Putnam, 1967.   A collection of many songs with words in both Spanish and English.   (B-D)

The Fireside Book of Folk Songs, new ed., ed. by Margaret B. Boni; illus. by Alice and Martin Provensen. Simon, 1966.   A standard favorite, now containing guitar chords for the many traditional songs.   (C-D)

Hi! Ho! The Rattlin' Bog, and Other Folk Songs for Group Singing, sel. by John Langstaff; illus. by Robin Jacques. Harcourt, 1969.   Ballads, sea chanteys, dance songs, and other musical treasures, collected by a well-known folksinger. Also try *Jim Along Josie,* comp. by Nancy and John Langstaff (Harcourt, 1970) and (for younger children) *Sweetly Sings the Donkey: Animal Rounds for Children to Sing or Play on Recorders* (A Margaret McElderry Book/Atheneum, 1976).   (A-D)

The Laura Ingalls Wilder Songbook: Favorite Songs from the Little House Books, ed. by Eugenia Garson and Herbert Haufrecht; illus. by Garth Williams. Harper, 1968.   A handsome book of music from frontier days.   (A-C)

Lullabies and Night Songs, ed. by William Engvick; music by Alec Wilder; illus. by Maurice Sendak. Harper 1965.   An inviting collection of traditional songs and nursery rhymes, with illustrations by the inimitable Sendak.   (B-C)

The Pooh Song Book, words by A. A. Milne; music by H. Fraser-Simson. Dutton, 1961.   "The Hums of Pooh," "The King's Breakfast," and fourteen songs from *When We Were Very Young.* Also includes a piano-vocal score.   (B-C)

Rockabye Baby: Lullabies of Many Lands and Peoples, comp. by Carl Miller. U.S. Committee for UNICEF, 1975. Paper. A pleasant way to share with young children the songs of other children like themselves. (A-B)

Songs and Stories from Uganda, by W. Moses Serwadda; illus. by Leo and Diane Dillon. Crowell, 1974. A handsome book of stories and songs to sing, dance, and play, illustrated with striking woodcuts. (C-D)

Songs of the Chippewa, ad. by John Bierhorst; illus. by Minja Park Kim. Farrar, 1974. Adapted from the collections of Frances Densmore and Henry Rowe Schoolcraft, with both Chippewa and English words. (B-D)

El Toro Pinto and Other Songs in Spanish, sel. and illus. by Anne Rockwell. Macmillan, 1971. An excellent collection of children's songs from Spain and Latin America with colorful illustrations. English text and guitar chords are included. (B-C)

Walk Together Children: Black American Spirituals, sel. and illus. by Ashley Bryan. Atheneum, 1974. Powerful woodcuts enhance this introduction to spirituals. (B-C)

Holiday Singing

American Folk Songs for Christmas, by Ruth P. Seeger; illus. by Barbara Cooney. Doubleday, 1953. Contains more than fifty American folk songs with Christmas themes. (A-C)

The Friendly Beasts, ad. by Laura Nelson Baker; illus. by Nicholas Sidjakov. Parnassus, 1957. An adaptation of the old English Christmas carol. (B-C)

The Holiday Song Book, ed. and illus. by Robert Quackenbush. Lothrop, 1977. Simple musical arrangements for both the piano and the guitar accompany the hundred songs for twenty-seven different holidays. A welcome collection for family gatherings. (B-C)

The Little Drummer Boy, illus. by Ezra Jack Keats. Macmillan, 1968. Paper, Collier/MacMillan. Beautiful pictures in glowing colors suggestive of the Holy Land convey the poignancy of this popular Christmas song. (★A-B)

On Christmas Day in the Morning! comp. by John Langstaff; illus. by Antony Groves-Raines. Harcourt, 1959. A Christmas book for all ages, this contains four well-known carols illustrated in a medieval style. (B-D)

Over the River and Through the Wood, by Lydia Maria Child; pictures by Brinton Turkle. Coward, 1974. Paper, Scholastic. Lively illustrations and the traditional verse celebrate Thanksgiving at Grandma's. An American classic. (A-B)

The Star-Spangled Banner, illus. by Peter Spier. Doubleday, 1973. The verses of our national anthem are interpreted in a large and inspiring picture book, with the music included. (B-D)

Animal Stories

The Call of the Wild, by Jack London; illus. by Charles Pickard. Macmillan, 1963. Paper, Scholastic. The story of a dog, brutalized by men in the Klondike, who joined a pack of wolves. (C-D)

Chipmunks on the Doorstep, written and illus. by Edwin Tunis. Crowell, 1971. The habits of chipmunks are observed, sketched, and described in detail by the author who used patience and peanuts to entice them to his doorstep. Beautifully illustrated with 70 full-color drawings. (C)

Hawk, I'm Your Brother, by Byrd Baylor; illus. by Peter Parnall. Scribner, 1976. Paper, Scholastic. Determined to learn to fly, a young Indian boy adopts a hawk hoping their kinship will bring him closer to his goal. Written in free verse and illustrated with stark, simple line drawings. (B)

Incident at Hawk's Hill, by Allan W. Eckert; illus. by John Schoenherr. Little, 1971. Paper, Dell/Yearling.   Ben, a shy, lonely, six-year-old boy, survives in the wilds for several months, cared for by a female badger. This story, for older children, is based upon an actual incident.   (C-D)

The Incredible Journey, by Sheila Burnford; illus. by Carl Burger. Atlantic/Little, 1961. Paper, Bantam.   A young Labrador retriever, a Siamese cat, and a very old English bull terrier, left with a family friend while their owners are abroad, make their way home across miles of Canadian wilderness.   (C-D)

The Jungle Book, by Rudyard Kipling; illus. by Fritz Eichenberg. Grosset, 1959. Paper, Airmont.   Here, in Kipling's magic prose, are Mowgli, the boy the wolves adopted; wise Bagheera, the black panther; the wicked tiger, Shere Khan; and other familiar animal characters.   (B-D)

King of the Wind, by Marguerite Henry; illus. by Wesley Dennis. Rand, 1948. Paper, Rand.   This horse story opens excitingly with Man o' War's last race, then goes back to the origin of the famous Arab strain in Europe and America. *Justin Morgan Had a Horse* (Rand, 1954. Paper, Rand) is the author's story of a pint-sized colt who became the father of the very first breed of American horses.   (B-C)

Lassie Come Home, 30th anniversary ed., by Eric M. Knight. Holt, 1971. Paper, Dell/Yearling.   The faithfulness of a dog to her young master is shown as the reader follows Lassie on her long journey back from northern Scotland to Joe's home in Yorkshire. Lassie had been sold because there was little money in the household, but her love and determination to return home brought better times for all concerned.   (B-D)

Manhattan Is Missing, by E. W. Hildick; illus. by Jan Palmer. Doubleday, 1969. Paper, Avon/Camelot.   A young English boy and his family sublet an apartment in New York City on the condition that they care for the owner's Siamese cat, which suddenly disappears.   (C)

The Midnight Fox, by Betsy Byars; illus. by Ann Grifalconi. Viking, 1968. Paper, Avon/Camelot.   Tom tracks a black fox to her kit in their den. The fox steals a turkey and Tom's Uncle Fred vows to kill it. Only Tom's courage saves it from certain destruction.   (C)

My Side of the Mountain, by Jean George. Dutton,1959. Paper, Dutton/ Anytime.   A teenage boy runs away from home to spend a year in the Catskills, where he lives in a hollowed-out tree, finds and prepares his food, makes his tools and clothing, and learns a great deal about plant and animal life in the woods.   (C)

Old One-Toe, by Michel-Aimé Baudouy; tr. by Marie Ponsot; illus. by Johannes Troyer. Harcourt, 1959.   A cunning fox raids local chicken houses and there ensues a battle of wits between One-Toe with his vixen and kits, four lively French children, and a man. (C)

Old Yeller, by Frederick Gipson; illus. by Carl Burger. Harper, 1956. Paper, Harper/Trophy.   A boy and his mongrel dog face the dangers of the Texas frontier territory, while the boy's father is away on a cattle drive in Kansas in the 1860s. A sequel to this simple, moving story is *Savage Sam* (Harper, 1962. Paper, Harper/ Trophy).   (C-D)

Owls in the Family, by Farley Mowat; illus. by Robert Frankenberg. Atlantic/Little, 1961.   Two owls, Wol and Weeps, turn a household upside down, outwit a dog, and terrorize a neighborhood in this humorous and realistic story of family life in Canada. (B-C)

Ponies of Mykillengi, by Lonzo Anderson; illus. by Adrienne Adams. Scribner, 1966.   The birth of a foal is a frightening experience for two children lost in an Iceland blizzard with their ponies. After an earthquake, a snowstorm, and a volcanic eruption they find their way home safely. Lovely illustrations add to the appeal of this story for the younger audience.   (B-C)

Rascal: A Memoir of a Better Era, by Sterling North; illus. by John Schoenherr. Dutton, 1963. Paper, Avon.   True stories of pets seldom reach the greatness of this boyhood remembrance of a year spent with a mischievous pet raccoon, half a century ago. (B-D)

Smoky, the Cowhorse, written and illus. by Will James. Scribner, 1926. Paper, Scribner/Willow Leaf Library.   Born on the range, Smoky works as a cow pony until he is stolen and mistreated. His cowboy friend finds him and restores him to health.   (C-D)

Tyto: The Odyssey of an Owl, by Glyn Frewer. Lothrop, 1977.   A fascinating life-cycle story of a barn owl, set in Wales, and its successful struggle for survival against unbelievable odds.   (B-C)

Wharf Rat, by Miska Miles; illus. by John Schoenherr. Atlantic/Little, 1972.   After an oil slick fouls the beach, a displaced rat finds haven on a freighter.   (B)

Where the Red Fern Grows, by Wilson Rawls. Doubleday,1961. Paper, Bantam.   Billy, Old Dan, and Little Ann become the finest coon hunting team in the Ozark hills of Oklahoma. After a mountain lion fatally wounds Old Dan, Little Ann loses her will to live. The red fern grows over the graves.   (C-D)

The Yearling, by Marjorie K. Rawlings; illus. by N. C. Wyeth. Scribner, 1939. Paper, Scribner/Willow Leaf Library.   A lonely boy and his pet deer fawn grow up in the Florida scrub country where hardship and tragedy beset the boy and his parents. A sensitive, poignant tale.   (C-D)

Family Stories

All-of-a-Kind Family, by Sydney Taylor; illus. by Helen John. Follet, 1951. Paper, Dell/Yearling.   The five daughters of a Jewish family living on New York's lower East Side during the 1900s enjoy holidays, borrow books from the library, and celebrate the arrival of a baby brother. Followed by: *More All-of-a-Kind Family* (Follett, 1954. Paper, Dell), *All-of-a-Kind Family Uptown* (Follett, 1958. Paper, Dell), and *All-of-a-Kind Family Downtown* (Follett, 1972. Paper, Dell).   (C)

Amifika, by Lucille Clifton; illus. by Thomas DiGrazia. Dutton, 1977.   A warm and gentle picture book in which a little black boy looks for a place to hide because he fears his father won't remember him after being away from home in the army.   (A-B)

And Leffe Was Instead of a Dad, by Kerstin Thorvall; tr. by F. L. Mirro. Bradbury, 1974. This short novel of a nine-year-old Swedish boy deals with the problems he faces when his unmarried mother invites an ex-convict to live with them. A forthright and compassionate story. (D)

And Now, Miguel, by Joseph Krumgold; illus. by Jean Charlot. Crowell, 1953. Paper, Apollo. The secret wish of Miguel, who lives in the sheep-raising country of New Mexico, is to go with the men when they take the sheep to summer pasture high up in the mountains. His wish is granted, but in such a way that Miguel is both happy and unhappy. A quiet story with interesting family relationships. (C-D)

Are You There God? It's Me, Margaret, by Judy Blume. Bradbury, 1970. Paper, Dell/Yearling. An eleven-year-old girl, Margaret, explores growing up problems such as religion, menstruation, and girl-boy relationships with her friends and her grandmother. (C)

Bedtime for Frances, by Russell Hoban; illus. by Garth Williams. Harper, 1960. Paper, Harper/Trophy. Frances thought of too many unusual things when she went to bed, just as all small children do. A warm and loving picture book, and one of a series about Frances, the lovable, willful, little badger, and her family. (A)

Blue Willow, by Doris Gates; illus. by Paul Lantz. Viking, 1940. Paper, Penguin/Puffin. Ten-year-old Janey Larkin has one treasure, a blue willow plate, and one burning desire, a permanent home. Through them her dream comes to fruition. A realistic and unsentimental portrayal of the plight of migrant families during the depression era. (C)

Caddie Woodlawn, by Carol R. Brink; illus. by Trina Schart Hyman. Macmillan, 1973. Paper, Collier/Macmillan. This story, full of the excitement and drama of pioneer times, is told through the adventures of a lively eleven-year-old girl who discovers that "folks keep growing from one person into another all their lives." (C)

Child of the Owl, by Laurence Yep. Harper, 1977. Paper, Dell/Laurel-Leaf. When her father becomes ill, Casey goes to live with her Chinese grandmother, Paw-Paw, in San Francisco. As Casey learns about her heritage, she comes to realize that Paw-Paw's home is her home, too. An unusual story of Chinese heritage. (C-D)

Daddy, by Jeannette Caines; illus. by Ronald Himler. Harper, 1977. A child of separated parents describes the special activities she shares with her father on Saturday. A simple, warm, and loving picture story.   (A)

Did You Carry the Flag Today, Charley? by Rebecca Caudill; illus. by Nancy Grossman. Holt, 1971. Paper, Holt/Owlet.   Independent, five-year-old Charley manages to receive the highest honor in school—being chosen to carry the flag because he is the most helpful. A delightful, realistic tale of the Appalachian hills. (A-B)

Duffy's Rocks, by Edward Fenton, Dutton, 1974.   Pittsburgh during the Depression is the setting for a story about an Irish American boy and his fruitless efforts to find his runaway father. An excellent picture of an Irish family in the 1930s.   (C-D)

The Edge of Nowhere, by Lucy J. Sypher; illus. by Ray Abel. Atheneum, 1972.   Lucy feels that nothing ever happens in North Dakota in 1916. However, she changes her mind after watching a fire in town, being snowbound with her brother, and making three new friends. Followed by *The Spell of the Northern Lights* (Atheneum, 1975) and *The Turnabout Year* (Atheneum, 1976).   (C)

Friday Night Is Papa Night, by Ruth Sonneborn; illus. by Emily McCully. Viking, 1970. Paper, Holt/Satellite.   This night is always a special occasion because Papa comes home. One time he arrives late, but with popsicles and presents for everyone. They agree that they need to celebrate. A picture story book.   (A)

The Half Sisters, by Natalie Savage Carlson; illus. by Tony DiGrazia. Harper, 1970. Paper, Harper/Trophy.   Luvy, eleven years old, wants to be grown up, yet longs to climb trees, play with dolls, and pretend to be a circus performer. A warm, family story which takes place in the early part of the twentieth century.   (B-C)

Hello, Aurora, by Anne-Catharina Vestly; tr. by Eileen Amos; illus. by Leonard Kestler. Crowell, 1974.   While mother works, Aurora, father, and baby Socrates manage the household very well, something neighbors have difficulty in understanding and accepting. Translated from the Norwegian. A sequel is *Aurora and Socrates.* (Crowell, 1977).   (C)

The Hundred Penny Box, by Sharon Bell Mathis; illus. by Diane and Leo Dillon. Viking, 1975.   Michael loves to hear the stories Aunt Dew tells from the hundred penny box. When Michael's mother wants to throw away the dilapidated old coin box, he protests. A warm story about the old and the young.   (B)

Jane, Wishing, by Tobi Tobias; illus. by Trina Schart Hyman. Viking, 1977.   Jane wished for long, red hair; a fancy name like Amanda or Melissa, sea green eyes, pale skin; and a beautiful smile. She didn't get them, but she decided she could be happy anyway.   (A-B)

The Little House in the Big Woods, by Laura Ingalls Wilder; illus. by Garth Williams. Harper, 1953. Paper, Harper/Trophy.   A pioneer family lives through pleasures and hardships in Wisconsin. There are howling winds, wild animals, and deep snows to contend with, but there is always the security of Ma's loving care and the gaiety of Pa's fiddle-playing. There are eight other books in the "Little House" series.   (B-C)

Little Women, by Louisa May Alcott; illus. by Barbara Cooney. Crowell, 1955. Paper, Penguin/Puffin.   Irrepressible Jo; frail, protected Beth; pretty, ambitious Amy; and sensible, responsible Meg, the oldest of the sisters, provide the focus for a family story which is full of action, pathos, humor, and real life.   (C-D)

M. C. Higgins the Great, by Virginia Hamilton. Macmillan, 1974. Paper, Dell/Yearling.   M. C. dreams of escape for himself and his family from a life of strip mining. From the top of a 40-foot pole, he examines past and future as well as family relationships until he comes to terms with his heritage.   (C-D)

Me and Mr. Stenner, by Evan Hunter. Lippincott, 1976. Paper, Dell/Yearling.   Abby finds herself caught in the middle after her mother's remarriage. She loves her father, but she also loves Mr. Stenner, the man her mother marries. This narrative explores change in a family's life with insight and humor.   (D)

Meet the Austins, by Madeleine L'Engle. Vanguard, 1960.   The ups and downs of a doctor's family are told by the twelve-year-old daughter during a year in which a spoiled young orphan comes to live with them. The Austins are as real as the family next door, facing happiness and sorrow with understanding and love.   (C)

The Moffats, by Eleanor Estes; illus. by Louis Slobodkin. Harcourt, 1941. Paper, Harcourt/Voyager.   Sylvie, Joey, Jane, and Rufus live with their mother in the yellow house on New Dollar Street. Their everyday adventures are always entertaining and often amusing. Sequels are *The Middle Moffat* (Harcourt, 1942. Paper, Harcourt/Voyager) and *Rufus M.* (Harcourt, 1943).   (B-C)

Mom, the Wolfman and Me, by Norma Klein. Pantheon, 1972. Paper, Avon/Camelot. Eleven-year-old Brett's life seems just right with her single mother. When Theo, nicknamed the Wolfman, comes along, Brett thinks of many reasons why her mother should not marry him or anyone else.   (C)

My Great-Grandfather, the Heroes, and I: A Brief Study of Heroes in Verse and Prose, Made Up and Told in Several Attic Rooms by My Great-Grandfather and I, by James Krüss, tr. by E. von Heyman. Atheneum, 1973.   When a young boy and an old man are invalids together, writing stories makes a great way to entertain each other. Translated from the German.   (C-D)

Naomi, by Berniece Rabe. Nelson, 1975. Paper, Bantam.   During the 1930s a Missouri farm girl is told by a fortune-teller that she will die before she is fourteen. This is a warm and human story of her thirteenth year as she lives trying to please God and family, and avoid her fate. *The Girl Who Had No Name* (Dutton, 1977. Paper, Bantam) is another unique story by this author in which Girlie discovers why she was not named at birth.   (C-D)

Nobody's Family Is Going to Change, written and illus. by Louise Fitzhugh. Farrar, 1974. Paper, Dell/Yearling.   Through a series of family disagreements over her seven-year-old brother's efforts to become a dancer and her own determination to be a lawyer, a black eleven-year-old girl realizes that it is up to children to take the initiative since parents rarely change.   (C)

Ordinary Jack: Being the First Part of the Bagthorpe Saga, by Helen Cresswell. Macmillan, 1977.   Jack is an ordinary boy in a talented family. With the help of Uncle Parker, he distinguishes himself as a prophet by having a series of faked visions. There are more stories about the Bagthorpes, the dog Zero, the grandparents, and their zany mishaps.   (C)

Queenie Peavy, by Robert Burch; illus. by Jerry Lazare. Viking, 1966.

Unhappy and rebellious because of her father's imprisonment, Queenie, a most likeable girl from the rural south, gradually comes to grips with reality.   (C)

Ramona and Her Father, by Beverly Cleary; illus. by Alan Tiegreen. Morrow, 1977. Paper, Dell/Yearling.   Both amusing and poignant is this account of seven-year-old Ramona's experiences when her father is suddenly jobless and she initiates a campaign to get him to stop smoking. There are other stories about Ramona, her family, and friends.   (B)

Roll of Thunder, Hear My Cry, by Mildred Taylor; illus. by Jerry Pinkney. Dial, 1976. Paper, Bantam.   The lives of Cassie and her family are made difficult by prejudice and discrimination, something the children find hard to understand as they fight to save the land that is theirs. Black family life in Mississippi during the Depression.   (C-D)

Stevie, written and illus. by John Steptoe. Harper, 1969.   Robert, a small boy, resents the presence of a house guest and wishes he would go away. A simple and moving picture book.   (B)

The Summer of the Swans, by Betsy Byars; illus. by Ted CoConis. Viking, 1970. Paper, Avon/Camelot.   Sara is engrossed in adolescent self-pity until her mentally retarded brother becomes lost while trying to find some swans he had seen earlier. Through this experience she develops insight into herself and her family.   (C)

Where the Lilies Bloom, by Vera and Bill Cleaver. Lippincott, 1969. Paper, New American Library.   After her father's death, fourteen-year-old Mary Call Luther becomes responsible for her brother and sister. Secretly she buries her father, and resourcefully she keeps the family together in their Appalachian mountain home.   (C-D)

A Year in the Life of Rosie Bernard, by Barbara Brenner; illus. by Joan Sandin. Harper, 1971. Paper, Avon/Camelot.   Rosie, motherless and living with relatives, has her life complicated when her actor father brings home a new wife. A humorous and warm portrait of family life in Brooklyn in the 1930s.   (C-D)

The Year of the Raccoon, by Lee Kingman. Houghton, 1966. Paper. Dell/Yearling.   Fifteen-year-old Joey, overwhelmed by a successful father and two talented brothers, considers himself the family failure. He develops assurance during a memorable year when he keeps a pet raccoon. (D)

Zeek Silver Moon, by Amy Erhlich; illus. by Robert Andrew Parker. Dial, 1972. Paper, Dial/Pied Piper. Everyday childhood events of the first four years of a boy's life are quietly illuminated with water-color pictures which depict the warmth and love of a traditional family. (A)

Friendship

Amos and Boris, by William Steig. Farrar, 1977. Paper, Penguin/ Puffin. An incongruous friendship ensues after Amos, the mouse, falls off his boat and is saved by Boris, the whale. A picture-book story. (B)

Bridge to Terabithia, by Katherine Paterson; illus. by Donna Diamond. Crowell, 1977. Paper, Avon/Camelot. Jess and Leslie become friends even though she beats him in a foot race. Together they reign supreme in a magical world of imagination and learning, Terabithia, until Leslie's sudden death. Other elements of friend-ship are explored in the author's *The Great Gilly Hopkins* (Crowell, 1978). (C)

Don't Hurt Laurie, by Willo D. Roberts; illus. by Ruth Sanderson. Atheneum, 1977. Laurie, physically abused, finds hope through her stepfather's family while her mother seeks medical help. (C-D)

Frog and Toad Together, by Arnold Lobel. Harper, 1972. Paper, Harper/Trophy. Five stories about these true friends include such human concerns as waiting for a garden to grow and trying not to eat one more cookie. Another easy-to-read story by Lobel is *Frog and Toad Are Friends* (Harper, 1970. Paper, Harper/Trophy). (A-B)

George and Martha, written and illus. by James Marshall. Houghton,

1972. Paper, Houghton/Sandpiper. Two huge hippopotamuses remain friends through the crises of misunderstanding about split pea soup, an invasion of privacy, and the loss of a tooth. Followed by *George and Martha Encore* (Houghton, 1973. Paper. Houghton/ Sandpiper), also in the same, tidy, picture-book format. (A-B)

A Girl Called Al, by Constance Greene; illus. by Byron Barton. Viking, 1969. Paper, Dell/Yearling. A seventh-grade girl, her slightly fat friend, and the assistant superintendent of their apartment building form a mutually needed friendship resulting in the usual and some unusual joys and sorrows. (C)

Growin', by Nikki Grimes; illus. by Charles Lilly. Dial, 1977. After her father dies, a black girl and her mother move to a new neighborhood where she forms an unlikely friendship with Jim Jim, the class bully. (B-C)

Jennifer, Hecate, Macbeth, William McKinley and Me, Elizabeth, by E. L. Konigsburg. Atheneum, 1967. Paper, Atheneum/Aladdin. Elizabeth feels she is the loneliest only child in New York City until she meets Jennifer, a young witch, who teaches Elizabeth all about witchcraft. (B-C)

Peter and Veronica, by Marilyn Sachs. Doubleday, 1969. Paper, Dell/ Yearling. A twelve-year-old Jewish boy struggles to maintain his friendship with his classmate, Veronica, despite the opposition of their parents and the disapproval of his older friends. (C)

Philip Hall Likes Me, I Reckon Maybe, by Bette Greene. Dial, 1974. Paper, Dell/Yearling. Beth, an energetic and spunky black girl, discovers her first love, Philip Hall. They capture chicken thieves, picket a local market, and compete in a calf-judging contest in rural Arkansas. (B-C)

Rosie and Michael, by Judith Viorst; illus. by Lorna Tomei. Atheneum, 1974. Paper, Atheneum/Aladdin. Rosie and Michael are friends even when he's dopey and she's grouchy. He sprays Koolwhip in her sneakers and she lets the air out of his basketball. A picture storybook. (B)

Thank You, Jackie Robinson, by Barbara Cohen; illus. by Richard Cuffari. Lothrop, 1974. The friendship of Sam, a fatherless white youth, and Davy, an elderly black man, is portrayed with warmth and candor. The characters have unusual depth and the story succeeds in conveying an understanding of friendship and death. (B-C)

Tony and Me, by Alfred Slote. Lippincott, 1974. Paper, Avon/Camelot. Tony, a star athlete, befriends Bill and gives hope to the losing baseball team, but Tony's shoplifting problems force Bill to make some tough decisions.   (C)

Very Far Away from Anywhere Else, by Ursula K. LeGuin. Atheneum, 1976. Paper, Bantam.   Seventeen-year-old Owen wants to become a scientist. Through the friendship of Natalie, who is dedicated to a music career, he sees how he can work toward his goal.   (D)

Humorous Stories

Abel's Island, written and illus. by William Steig. Farrar, 1976. Paper, Bantam.   Carried off by flood waters and separated from his bride, Abel the mouse exhibits great powers of survival despite his pampered background.   (B)

And to Think That I Saw It on Mulberry Street, written and illus. by Dr. Seuss. Vanguard, 1937.   A small boy's imagination conjures up an amazing parade, bit by bit, inspired by the sight of a "plain horse and wagon on Mulberry Street." Another comic suspense tale by this well-known humorist, also in picture-book format, is the *500 Hats of Bartholomew Cubbins,* (Vanguard, 1938).   (A)

Ben and Me, written and illus. by Robert Lawson. Little, 1939. Paper, Dell/Yearling.   The memoirs of Amos, the mouse, reveal his role in Ben Franklin's life and present the great man in an unusual, if not very heroic, light. A spoof on history.   (B-C)

The Best Christmas Pageant Ever, by Barbara Robinson, Harper, 1972. Paper, Avon/Camelot.   A family of six children, with a reputation for being the worst kids in the history of the world, find a totally new experience after they volunteer to take part in the Christmas Nativity play. Funny and fast-paced. (B-C)

The Case of the Elevator Duck, by Polly B. Berends; illus. by James Washburn. Random, 1973. Paper, Dell/Yearling. Young Gilbert disobeys the housing project edict about pets when he finds a lost duck on the elevator in his building. (B)

The Complete Nonsense Book, by Edward Lear; ed. by Lady Strachey. Dodd, 1948. Paper, Dover. "Containing all the original pictures and verses, together with new material," is the subtitle of this now classic volume. (B-C)

The Complete Peterkin Papers, by Lucretia P. Hale, Houghton, 1960. The daily catastrophes of the Victorian Peterkin family continue to amuse today's audiences who know better than to put salt in their coffee or to play a piano out of doors during winter. (B-D)

Danny, the Champion of the World, by Roald Dahl; illus. by Jill Bennett. Knopf, 1975. Paper, Bantam. A British view of the landed rich is afforded in this tale of a boy and his father and their dangerous delight in poaching. For older children. (C-D)

The Dog Who Wouldn't Be, by Farley Mowat; illus. by Paul Galdone. Atlantic/Little, 1957. Paper, BJ/Jove. A delightfully funny story of a dog and his boy. Mutt is a dog of remarkable character and personality, and often proves himself to be more human than dog. (C)

Dreams of Victory, by Ellen Conford; illus. by Gail Rockwell. Little, 1973. Paper, Dell/Yearling. Imagination proves to be the key to Victory's eventual success after all her dreams about becoming the first woman president, astronaut, or even Miss Universe.

Elvis and His Friends, by Maria Gripe; with drawings by Harald Gripe. Seymour Lawrence/Delacorte, 1976. In this sequel to *Elvis and His Secret* (Seymour Lawrence/Delacorte, 1976), Elvis starts school, achieves better understanding, and gains greater acceptance by his mother. (C)

The Enormous Egg, by Oliver Butterworth; illus. by Louis Darling. Little, 1956. Paper, Dell/Yearling. A twelve-year-old boy meets unexpected problems when he finds an egg which hatches out a dinosaur capable of growing to an immense size. (B-C)

Fat Men from Space, by Daniel Manus Pinkwater. Dodd, 1977. William's tooth radio conveys news about the spacemen who are coming to eat all of the world's junk food. For younger readers. *Lizard Music* (Dodd, 1976. Paper, Dell/Yearling) reveals on television a lizard band which tells the hero of a little-known invasion from outer space.   (C)

Figgs and Phantoms, written and illus. by Ellen Raskin. Dutton, 1974. Paper, Dutton/Anytime.   Mona Lisa Newton and her strange family have a heaven of their own in this witty and most original story. More humor and adventure may be found in *The Mysterious Disappearance of Leon (I Mean Noel),* (Dutton, 1971. Paper, Dutton/ Anytime), which involves the reader in Caroline Carillon's antic search for her missing husband.   (C-D)

The Ghost Belonged to Me: A Novel, by Richard Peck. Viking, 1975. Paper, Avon/Camelot.   The Mississippi River Valley at the turn of the century provides a pleasant backdrop for a story of the strange happenings and adventures of a skeptical boy who encounters a young female ghost.   (C-D)

Henry Huggins, by Beverly Cleary; illus. by Louis Darling. Morrow, 1950. Paper, Dell/Yearling.   Henry is a typical small boy who gets himself into one amusing predicament after another. The adventures of this very real boy and his friends are continued in *Henry and Beezus* (Morrow, 1952. Paper, Dell/Yearling); *Henry and Ribsy* (Morrow, 1954. Paper, Dell/Yearling); *Henry and the Paper Route* (Morrow, 1957. Paper, Dell/Yearling); *Henry and the Clubhouse* (Morrow, 1962. Paper, Dell/Yearling); *Ribsy* (Morrow, 1964. Paper, Dell/Yearling).   (B-C)

Henry Reed, Inc., by Keith Robertson; illus. by Robert McCloskey. Viking, 1958. Paper, Dell/Yearling.   An ingenious young boy gives a straightforward episodic account of his hilarious summer enterprises. More laughs can be found in *Henry Reed's Journey* (Viking, 1963) and *Henry Reed's Baby-Sitting Service* (Viking, 1966).   (C)

Homer Price, written and illus. by Robert McCloskey. Viking, 1943. Paper, Penguin/Puffin.   Homer's acquaintances from the barbershop and the doughnut shop find themselves in extremely funny predicaments. Small-town America with a tall-tale flavor.   (B-C)

Isabelle the Itch, by Constance C. Green; illus. by Emily McCully.

Viking, 1973. Paper, Dell/Yearling. Energetic Isabelle begins to learn that if she channels her energy she can "scale mountains." (C)

Mary Poppins, by P. L. Travers; illus. by Mary Shepard. Harcourt, 1934. Paper, Harcourt/Voyager. Mary Poppins blew in on an east wind and left on a west wind. In between she changed the lives of the Banks family, especially Jan and Michael who enjoyed strange and amusing adventures with this extraordinary nursemaid. She returns in *Mary Poppins Comes Back* (Harcourt, 1934. Paper, Harcourt/Voyager); *Mary Poppins Opens the Door* (Harcourt, 1943. Paper, Harcourt/Voyager); and in *Mary Poppins in the Park* (Harcourt, 1952. Paper, Harcourt/Voyager). (A-B)

Mister Popper's Penguins, by Richard and Florence Atwater; illus. by Robert Lawson. Little, 1938. Paper, Dell/Yearling. A paperhanger's interest in polar exploration leads to a donation of penguins and the unexpected alteration of the Popper family's way of life. (B-C)

Pippi Longstocking, by Astrid Lindgren; illus. by Louis B. Glanzman. Viking 1950. Paper, Penguin/Puffin. Pippi is a most remarkable nine-year-old girl who lives alone, except for a monkey and a horse. Her fantastic stories and escapades are shared by the children next door. Followed by *Pippi Goes on Board,* (Viking, 1957) and *Pippi in the South Seas* (Viking, 1959). (B)

A Proud Taste for Scarlet and Miniver, by E. L. Konigsburg. Atheneum, 1971. Paper, Atheneum/Aladdin. The story of Eleanor of Aquitaine is told from her position on a cloud in heaven while she and her friends await the admission of Henry II. Entertaining fare for older children. (C-D)

Tales of a Fourth Grade Nothing, by Judy Blume; illus. by Roy Doty. Dutton, 1972. Paper, Dell/Yearling. A lighthearted look at the problems of Peter, his four-year-old brother, and the outrageous situations which develop. (B)

The Toothpaste Millionaire, written by Jean Merrill. Houghton, 1972. At twelve, Rufus Mayflower, a black in an East Cleveland neighborhood, puts his mathematical and business genius to work with the help of Kate, his new friend from an Eastern suburb. *The Pushcart*

War (Addison, 1964. Paper, Dell) is another favorite by this author. (C)

Winnie-the-Pooh, new ed., by A. A. Milne; illus. by E. H. Shepard. Dutton, 1961. Paper, Dell/Yearling. Affection, wit, and style mark this modern classic about Pooh, Piglet, and Christopher Robin. The companion book, *The House at Pooh Corner* (new ed. Dutton, 1961. Paper, Dell/Yearling) introduces Tigger and a hilarious hunt for Heffalumps. (A-C)

Mystery and Suspense

Adventures of the Black Hand Gang, by Hans Jurgen Press; tr. by Barbara Littlewood. Prentice, 1977. Active, perceptive involvement by the reader in identifying picture clues adds to the enjoyment of an unusual book. (C)

Baby Needs Shoes, by Dale Carlson; illus. by Victoria de Larrea. Atheneum, 1974. Janet knew she was not "too normal a person." She played the guitar without taking lessons and she could predict numbers, which meant she earned a lot of money working for Fat Charlie's floating crap games. (D)

Basil of Baker Street, by Eve Titus; illus. by Paul Galdone. McGraw, 1963. Paper, Archway. Scientific detection on a small scale as practiced by Basil, the famous mouse detective, narrated by his friend, companion, and admirer, Dr. David Q. Dawson. A pleasing introduction for the young reader to this genre of literature. (B-C)

The Boy's Sherlock Holmes, new and enl. ed., by Arthur Conan Doyle. Harper, 1961. In spite of its sexist title, this edition remains the most appealing one for introducing readers to the famed sleuth. Illustrated with atmospheric photographs. (C-D)

The Court of the Stone Children, by Eleanor Cameron. Dutton, 1973.

Paper, Avon. Dominique of the French Chateau's past seeks the help of Nina of the present in unraveling a mystery dormant since the time of Napoleon. (C)

The Dollhouse Caper, by Jean S. O'Connell; illus. by Erik Blegvad. Crowell, 1976. Paper, Scholastic. A dollhouse family witnesses an attempted burglary and worries that the children of the human family have outgrown them. A light mystery with comic touches, of appeal to the younger child. (B)

The Egypt Game, by Zilpha K. Snyder; with drawings by Alton Raible. Atheneum, 1967. Paper, Atheneum/Aladdin. A heterogeneous group of children imaginatively create their own Egypt in a desolate storage yard, attracting the attention of a murderer. (B-C)

Five Boys in a Cave, by Richard Church. Day, 1951. A tale full of adventure and excitement presents minute details of the hazardous experiences of the five members of the Tomahawk Secret Society as they explore an unknown cave. (B-C)

From the Mixed Up Files of Mrs. Basil E. Frankweiler, written and illus. by E. L. Konigsburg. Atheneum, 1967. Paper, Atheneum/ Aladdin. Runaways Claudia and Jamie Kincaid take up residence in the Metropolitan Museum of Art and discover the solution to a mystery. (C)

Go to the Room of the Eyes, by Betty K. Erwin; illus. by Irene Burns. Little, 1969. The six Evans children are dubious about moving into the big, old, city house until Susan discovers the first clue in a treasure hunt laid by children who had lived there thirty years before. For older children. (C)

Goody Hall, story and pictures by Natalie Babbitt. Farrar, 1971. Paper, Avon/Camelot. Is Midas Goody really buried in the stone tomb on the grounds of the Goody Hall family mansion? His son Willet refuses to admit he is, so Hercules Feltwright, actor turned tutor, tries to learn the secret. (C)

The Ice Ghosts Mystery, by Jane L. Curry. A Margaret K. McElderry Book/Atheneum, 1972. Paper, Atheneum/Aladdin. No one in Professor Bird's family believes he was really swept away by an avalanche. Mab, Perry, Oriole, and their determined mother fly to the Austrian Alps to find the ice ghosts who imperil the world. (C)

The Ides of April, by Mary Ray. Farrar, 1975.   The real murderer of Senator Caius Pomponius must be discovered or all his slaves will die.   (C-D)

The Intruder, by John Rowe Townsend. Lippincott, 1970. Paper, Dell/ Laurel Leaf.   Who is the real Arnold Haithwaite? Young Arnold grapples with personal identity, class distinctions, and attempted murder in a British mystery with a sensitively drawn seaside setting.   (C-D)

The Inway Investigators; or, The Mystery at McCracken's Place, by Jane W. Yolen; illus. by Allan Eitzen. Paper, Archway.   "The two i's of the Inway Investigation are always open—for trouble."   (D)

The Mystery of the Missing Red Mitten, written and illus. by Steven Kellogg. Dial, 1974. Paper, Dial/Pied Piper.   Annie searches for the fifth mitten she has lost in a single winter in a picture story which will hold the attention of young children.   (A)

Nate the Great, by Marjorie W. Sharmat; illus. by Marc Simont. Coward, 1972. Paper, Dell/Yearling.   Exploits of a young detective who sleuths alone. This is the first in a series and is followed by *Nate the Great Goes under Cover* (Coward, 1974) and *Nate the Great and the Phony Clue* (Coward, 1977).   (B)

Night Fall, by Joan Aiken. Holt, 1971. Paper, Dell/Yearling.   A terrifying dream haunts Meg Frazier until she returns to the Cornish seaside town where reality turned nightmare for a small child.   (C)

No Way of Telling, by Emma Smith. A Margaret K. McElderry Book/ Atheneum, 1972.   Snowbound Amy and her grandmother encounter a series of strange intruders.   (C-D)

The Real Thief, written and illus. by William Steig. Farrar, 1973. Paper, Dell/Yearling.   Gawain, the goose guard of the Royal Treasury, flies away when falsely accused of theft. A picture story by the noted cartoonist.   (B)

The Remarkable Return of Winston Potter Crisply, by Eve Rice. Greenwillow, 1978.   Mother keeps sending money to brilliant brother Winston at Harvard, but Max and Becky see and shadow him as he slinks around New York in disguise.   (C)

The Secret Garden, by Frances H. Burnett; illus. by Tasha Tudor. Lippincott, 1962. Paper, Dell/Yearling.   Time has not dimmed the appeal of this story of three children whose lives are changed by the discovery and development of the garden on the other side of the wall.   (C)

Toby, Granny and George, by Robbie Branscum; illus. by Glen Rounds. Doubleday, 1975. Paper, Avon/Camelot.   Toby reckoned that Deacon Treat, Pa of the missing baby, was "the meanest man she ever seen." But, when he was found in the baptizing hole, not drowned but shot with a twenty-two, she couldn't help wonder who did it. Then someone shot at her!   (C)

The View from the Cherry Tree, by Willo Davis Roberts. Atheneum, 1975. Paper, Atheneum/Aladdin.   Rob had a bad habit of exaggerating, so when he saw a murder no one believed him but the murderer.   (C)

The Westing Game, written and illus. by Ellen Raskin. Dutton, 1978. Offbeat verbal sleight of mind combines word puzzles and a murderer's trail with memorable characters. There is also a collection of short mysteries by this author called *The Tattoed Potato and Other Clues* (Dutton, 1975).   (C)

Historical Fiction

Across Five Aprils, by Irene Hunt. Follett, 1964. Paper, Grosset/Tempo.   The years of the Civil War are experienced by a ten-year-old boy and his family in southern Illinois. Battle and campaign details are described by his older brothers who are fighting on opposite sides.   (C)

The Adventures of Tom Sawyer, by Mark Twain; illus. by John Falter. Macmillan, 1962. Paper, Penguin/Puffin.   The activities of Tom and his friends in a nineteenth-century Missouri River town reveal the lively and sometimes seamy side of village life. Its sequel, *The*

Adventures of Huckleberry Finn (Macmillan, 1962. Paper, Penguin/Puffin), has been claimed by children and adults; some consider it "the great American novel."   (C-D)

The Apple and the Arrow, by Mary and Conrad Buff. Houghton, 1941. Paper, Houghton/Sandpiper.   The year is 1292 when the story of Switzerland's revolt against Austria takes place. The tale of William Tell's leadership is seen from the point of view of the young son from whose head, according to legend, the apple was shot.   (B)

A Boy of Old Prague, by Sulamith Ish-Kishor; illus. by Ben Shahn. Pantheon, 1963.   In the days of the feudal system of sixteenth-century Europe, Tomas, a peasant boy, is forced to spend time with a family in the feared Jewish ghetto.   (C)

The Boy without a Name, by Penelope Lively; illus. by Ann Dalton. Parnassus, 1975.   When an orphan boy arrives in Swinfield, England, all he knows is that he was born there in 1634, and he wants to find who his people really were. A brief story.   (B)

Call It Courage, written and illus. by Armstrong Sperry. Macmillan, 1940. Paper, Collier/Macmillan.   Mafatu, the son of a great Polynesian chief, proves his courage by conquering his fear of the sea. (B-C)

The Caves of the Great Hunters, by Hans Baumann; illus. with reproductions of cave paintings. Pantheon, 1962.   A fascinating, illustrated account of the accidental discovery by four schoolboys of Ice Age cave paintings in France. True and exciting.   (C)

The Door in the Wall, written and illus. by Marguerite de Angeli. Doubleday, 1949. Paper, Doubleday.   Robin, a boy with a physical disability, acquires courage and swims across the moat in the fog to gain assistance during a siege of the castle in this story of medieval London.   (B-C)

Dragonwings, by Laurence Yep. Harper, 1975. Paper, Harper/Trophy. Windrider's dream of flying is doubted by his fellow Chinese but not by his adolescent son who has the faith and energy to help his father make a flying machine. This story is set in early twentieth-century San Francisco, before, during, and after the great earthquake.   (C-D)

Fireweed, by Jill Paton Walsh. Farrar, 1970. Paper, Avon. An adolescent boy and girl, in London during the heavy World War II bombing, find each other and try to be responsible for their own lives during a strange, horrible, and special time. (C-D)

Friedrich, by Hans Richter; trans. from the German by Edite Kroll. Holt, 1970. The persecution of the Jews in Hitler's Germany is shown in this story of the friendship and anguish of two German boys, one of them Jewish. *I Was There* (Holt, 1972) continues the story of the young German boy's participation in the Hitler youth movement. (C-D)

Hakon of Rogen's Saga, by Erik Haugaard; illus. by Leo and Diane Dillon. Houghton, 1963. Paper, Houghton/Sandpiper. Set in Norway at the end of the Viking period, this haunting story is a first-person account of thirteen-year-old Hakon's struggle to regain his birthright. Followed by *A Slave's Tale* (Houghton, 1965). (C-D)

Hew against the Grain, by Betty Cummings. Atheneum, 1977. The loyalties of the Repas family of Virginia are split during the Civil War; each person, at home or at the front, is afflicted by his or her own particular hurt and must cope with the threat of a dwindling spirit. For mature children. (D)

Hitty: Her First Hundred Years, by Rachel Field; illus. by Dorothy Lathrop. Macmillan, 1937. A doll, six-and-a-half inches high and carved from mountain ash, has many narrow escapes over the years, from capture by crows to repose in an antique shop window. (B)

I, Juan de Pareja, by Elizabeth Borten de Treviño. Farrar, 1965. Paper, Dell/Yearling. An historical novel based on the life of a freed African slave who served Velasquez and became an artist in his own right. (C)

Island of the Blue Dolphins, by Scott O'Dell. Houghton, 1960. Paper, Dell/Yearling. An Indian girl, alone on a California island for eighteen years, makes a life for herself that has beauty and dignity. For older children. (C-D)

Johnny Tremain, by Esther Forbes. Houghton, 1943. Paper, Dell/Yearling Books. An apprentice to a silversmith has an accident which maims his hand. No longer able to work at his craft, he becomes involved in Boston's pre-Revolutionary activities. A traditional view of American history.   (C-D)

The Master Puppeteer, by Katherine Paterson; illus. by Haru Wells. Crowell, 1975.   Jiro, thirteen, is the son of a puppet maker, and an apprentice in a company of puppeteers. They mysteriously have enough to eat, but all around them is the poverty, hunger, and discontent of eighteenth-century Japan.   (C-D)

My Brother Sam Is Dead, by James and Christopher Collier. Four Winds, 1974. Paper, Scholastic.   When Sam is falsely accused of stealing his own cattle and is executed as an example of General Putnam's discipline, one can see that injustices are often inflicted upon the innocent in time of war, even during the American Revolution.   (C)

An Old Tale Carved Out of Stone, by A. Linevski; tr. by Maria Polushkin. Crown, 1973.   In the seventeenth and eighteenth centuries in Siberia, tribes were discovered who lived virtually in the Stone Age. This is a story of those people, especially Lio, who is forced to be the spiritual leader of his people when he is still young and inexperienced.   (C-D)

On the Day Peter Stuyvesant Sailed into Town, written and illus. by Arnold Lobel. Harper, 1971.   Told in rhyme, this is the story of the irascible governor's successful efforts to clean up New Amsterdam. The many brightly colored pictures are reminiscent of Dutch tiles.   (A-B)

Petros' War, by Alki Zei; tr. by Edward Fenton. Dutton, 1972.   Petros is ten years old when the Italians and Germans occupy Athens during World War II. He changes his ideas as to what constitutes a hero as he works for the underground and sees sadness and poverty all around him.   (C)

Roller Skates, by Ruth Sawyer; illus. by Angelo Valenti. Viking. 1936. Paper, Dell/Yearling.   New York City in the 1890s is the scene of Lucinda's never-to-be-forgotten tenth year, as she explores the city on roller skates.   (B)

The Samurai and the Long-Nosed Devils, by Lensey Namioka. McKay, 1976. Paper, Dell/Yearling.   Two ronin use their wits as well as their swords as they attempt to keep a group of merchants and missionaries from being harassed during the warlord's drive to unify sixteenth-century Japan. For an older audience.   (C-D)

The Slave Dancer, by Paula Fox. Bradbury, 1973. Paper, Dell/ Yearling.   When Jessie, a thirteen-year-old white boy, is captured in New Orleans and made to join the crew of a slave ship, he experiences the shock of human degradation which engulfs everyone connected with slavery.   (C-D)

Smith, by Leon Garfield; illus. by A. Maitland. Pantheon, 1967.   A twelve-year-old pickpocket becomes, much to his surprise, involved with a mysterious document and a murder. A fast-paced, colorfully written tale of eighteenth-century London.   (C-D)

Sounder, by William Armstrong; illus. by James Barkley. Harper, 1969. Paper, Harper/Trophy.   When a black sharecropper is thrown into jail for stealing a ham for his hungry family, his hunting dog Sounder is cruelly wounded by the sheriff. The dog doesn't bay again until years later, when his master returns. Set in the southern United States at the turn of the century.   (C-D)

The Summer of My German Soldier, by Bette Greene. Dial, 1973. Paper, Bantam.   Twelve-year-old Jewish Patty Bergen becomes friend of Anton, a German prisoner of war, in Arkansas during the second World War. He is the only one in her world who regards her as a "a person of value."   (C-D)

This Time, Tempe Wick? by Patricia Gauch; illus. by Margot Tomes. Coward, 1974.   When the soldiers mutiny and steal from the very farmers who have helped them, feisty Temperance Wick hides her horse in her bedroom and will not stand for the behavior of the rude soldiers. Based on a real incident in the Revolutionary War, this has special appeal for the younger child.   (B)

Thy Friend, Obadiah, written and illus. by Brinton Turkle. Viking, 1969. Paper, Penguin/Puffin.   A small Quaker boy who lives in Nantucket acquires a seagull friend which he doesn't value until later. In this, and other stories about Obadiah, the flavor of old Nantucket is given in the line and gouache pictures.   (A)

Time of Trial, by Hester Burton; illus. by Victor G. Ambrus. Philomel, 1964. Paper, Dell/Yearling. During the seventeenth century, seventeen-year-old Margaret, the daughter of a London bookseller, is sent to prison for advocating social reform and for printing a book judged to be inflammatory. (C-D)

Tituba of Salem Village, by Ann Petry. Crowell, 1964. A young slave in Salem, Massachusetts, is accused of witchcraft. Throughout the accusations and the famous trial, she shows great fortitude and strength of character. (C-D)

Treasure Island, by Robert Louis Stevenson; illus. by John Falter. Macmillan, 1963. Paper, Penguin/Puffin. Originally published in 1883, this is the suspenseful story of Long John Silver and his pirate crew who were led by a map to find treasure. (C-D)

The Upstairs Room, by Johanna Reiss. Crowell, 1972. Paper, Bantam. An account of a Jewish author's own experiences when she and her sister were hidden by a Dutch farm family during World War II. A story of the reactions of people in close confinement and secrecy—the tension and fear and the moments of humor and love. (B-C)

Walk the World's Rim, by Betty Baker. Harper, 1965. Paper, Harper/ Trophy. While accompanying Cabeza de Vaca and two Spanish companions searching for the gold of Cibola, an Indian boy matures as he learns to value the friendship of the slave Esteban and to question the ethics and loyalties of the Spanish captors. A story of the Southwest in the sixteenth century. (C-D)

When Hitler Stole Pink Rabbit, by Judith Kerr. Coward, 1972. Paper, Dell/Yearling. A Jewish family barely escapes from Germany before World War II, leaving their house and many possessions, including "pink rabbit" to Hitler and his soldiers. The important thing in this story is the family solidarity. (B-C)

White Bird, by Clyde Robert Bulla; illus. by Leonard Weisgard. Crowell, 1966. Running away finally proves to John Thomas, an orphan, that there is good in people and especially in Luke, the harsh, independent man who has brought him up. Set during pioneer days in Tennessee. (B)

The Witch of Blackbird Pond, by Elizabeth Speare. Houghton, 1958. Paper, Dell/Yearling. High-spirited Kit is a misfit in the stern Puritan household of her aunt and uncle. When she befriends a Quaker woman who is accused of being a witch, Kit, too, is suspect. (C)

The Wonderful Winter, by Marchette Chute. Dutton, 1954. Robin, who has run away to London, is befriended by some actors in Shakespeare's theater, and is taken into the loving home of the famous John Hemming. (C)

The Year of the Three-Legged Deer, by Eth Clifford; illus. by Richard Cuffari. Houghton, 1971. Paper, Dell/Yearling. It is the year 1819 in Indiana when a wounded fawn comes to the home of Jesse Benton, a white trader, his Indian wife, and their two children. It is also the year that Jesse buys the freedom of a black slave and encounters bitter racial hatred. (C)

Fantasy

The Adventures of Pinocchio, by Carlo Collodi; illus. by Attilio Mussino. Macmillan, 1972. Paper. The mischievous puppet whose nose grows longer every time he tells a lie is as loved here as he is in Italy where the classic story originated. This beautiful edition with illustrations by Attilio Mussino has been reissued as a paperback that is published by Macmillan. (B)

Alice's Adventures in Wonderland and Through the Looking Glass, by Lewis Carroll; illus. by John Tenniel. Macmillan, 1963. Paper, Penguin/Puffin. This is the well-known story of Alice and the White Rabbit whom she followed down a rabbit hole to a series of adventures. (B-C)

The Animal Family, by Randall Jarrell; illus. by Maurice Sendak. Pantheon, 1965. Paper, Dell/Yearling. A lonely hunter gathers an extraordinary family—a mermaid, a bear, a lynx, and a shipwrecked boy—in this gently written fantasy. The book is handsome in format with quiet illustrations. (B)

Below the Root, by Zilpha K. Snyder; illus. by Alton Raible. Atheneum, 1975. An ancient tree both nourishes and protects a civilization from a secret fate. The first of a series of three unusual fantasies. (C)

The Book of Three, by Lloyd Alexander. Holt, 1964.   Taran, would-be hero and assistant pig-keeper, assembles a group of companions to rescue the oracular pig, Hen wen, from the forces of evil. The first book in the author's Prydain Chronicles, which comprise five titles, it is followed by *The Black Cauldron* (Holt, 1965. Paper, Dell/Yearling); *The Castle of Llyr* (Holt, 1966. Paper, Dell/Yearling); *Taran Wanderer* (Holt, 1967. Paper, Dell/Yearling); and *The High King* (Holt, 1968).   (C-D)

The Borrowers, by Mary Norton; illus. by Beth and Joe Krush. Harcourt, 1953. Paper, Harcourt/Voyager.   A delightful fantasy filled with humor and suspense about a family of tiny people who live under the floor of an English country house and "borrow" what they need for daily living. Other books about Pod, Homily, and Arrietty are *The Borrowers Afield* (Harcourt, 1955. Paper, Harcourt/Voyager); *The Borrowers Afloat* (Harcourt, 1959. Paper, Harcourt/Voyager); and the *Borrowers Aloft* (Harcourt, 1961. Paper, Harcourt/Voyager).   (B-C)

Charlotte's Web, by E. B. White; illus. by Garth Williams. Harper, 1952. Paper, Harper/Trophy.   A little girl, Fern, saves a runt pig's life in the beginning, but it is Charlotte, a spider, able to write messages in her spider web, who saves Wilbur's life the second time and brings him fame and honor. *Stuart Little* (Harper, 1945. Paper, Harper/Trophy), an earlier book by this writer, chronicles the adventures of a tiny mouse.   (B)

The Children of Green Knowe, by Lucy M. Boston; illus. by Peter Boston. Harcourt, 1955. Paper, Harcourt/Voyager.   Tolly visits his great-grandmother at Green Knowe and discovers he can share the adventures of other children who in centuries past have lived in this old English country house. There are four other stories about Green Knowe when you have finished this one.   (B)

The Cricket in Times Square, by George Selden; illus by Garth Williams. Farrar, 1960. Paper, Dell/Yearling.   When he arrives at the Bellini newsstand in the Times Square subway station, the small black cricket from Connecticut is just a dirty "bug" to Mama Bellini, an interesting new friend for Tucker Mouse and Harry Cat, and a special pet for Mario.   (B)

The Daybreakers, written by Jane L. Curry; illus. by Charles Robinson. Harcourt, 1970.   A present-day brother and sister, who are black, and their white friend embark on some dangerous time-travel adventures with pre-Columbian people. Set in a West Virginian milltown. (B)

Dominic, written and illus. by William Steig. Farrar, 1972. Paper, Dell/Yearling. The adventures of a traveling dog who befriends the weak makes a delightful animal fantasy. (B)

Dragonsong, by Anne McCaffrey. Atheneum, 1976. Paper, Bantam, 1977. Menolly's love of harping is contrary to tradition, but her daring leads to conflict with the dangerous thread spores from which only the dragons of Pern are safe. Followed by *Dragonsinger* (Atheneum, 1977). (C-D)

Earthfasts, by William Mayne. Dutton, 1966. When an eighteenth-century drummer boy emerges with his candle from a mound on the English moors, adventures begin for two boys. This original story melds a range of time, the supernatural, legend, and folklore of the present day. (C-D)

Five Children and It, reprint of 1902 ed., by E. Nesbit. British Book Centre, 1974. Paper, Penguin/Puffin. When It, the prehistoric sand-fairy, grants five children their wishes, awkward results occur. There are two sequels to this long-time English favorite. (B)

Fog Magic, by Julia L. Sauer; illus. by Lynd Ward. Viking, 1943. Paper, Archway. Greta, who loves the fog, lives in two worlds — the real world of Little Village and that of Blue Cove Village, which existed over a hundred years ago. (B)

The Glassblower's Children, by Maria Gripe. Delacorte, 1973. Paper, Dell/Yearling. The two children of Albert, the glassblower, and Sofia, his wife, have been stolen from them. The magical touch in their lives appears in the character of Flutter Mildweather. (B)

Half Magic, by Edward Eager; illus. by N. M. Bodecker. Harcourt, 1954. Paper, Harcourt/Voyager. When Jane finds an unusual coin which grants half of any wish, strange and humorous adventures begin for her and her family. Further magical happenings are described in *Magic by the Lake* (Harcourt, 1957). (B)

Higglety Pigglety Pop! or, There Must be More to Life, written and illus. by Maurice Sendak. Harper, 1967. Jennie, the Sealyham, has everything, but she feels there is more to life than luxury and sets out to find its true meaning. Text and illustrations are combined perfectly in an unusual fantasy. (B)

The Hobbit, or There and Back Again, written and illus. by John R. R. Tolkien. Houghton, 1938. Paper, Ballantine. Bilbo Baggins, a most conventional hobbit, becomes involved in an unconventional adventure with dwarfs and a dragon when a wandering wizard stops at his door one morning. A good read-aloud book for families who enjoy adventure mixed with fantasy. (C-D)

The House with a Clock in Its Walls, by John Bellairs; pictures by Edward Gorey. Dial, 1973. Paper, Dell/Yearling. His uncle's wizardry is a source of amusement and danger for Lewis. A delightful mix of fantasy and humor. (B-C)

Journey Outside, by Mary Q. Steele; illus. by Rocco Negri. Viking, 1969. Paper, Penguin/Puffin. People who live in darkness travel a circular journey on an underground river. One boy finds his way outside and tries to learn as much as possible so he can ultimately lead his people to the Better Place. (B)

The Kelpie's Pearls, new ed., by Mollie Hunter; with drawings by Stephen Gammell. Harper, 1976. An old woman who lives alone in the Scottish Highlands becomes suspect when she befriends a water sprite and exhibits unusual skills which the townspeople interpret as witchcraft. (C)

The Lion, the Witch and the Wardrobe, by C. S. Lewis; illus. by Pauline Baynes. Macmillan, 1950. Paper, Collier/Macmillan. Peter, Susan, Edmond, and Lucy have exciting adventures in the land of Narnia which exists just beyond the vast reaches of a big wardrobe. These adventures continue in *Prince Caspian* (Macmillan, 1951. Paper, Collier/Macmillan); *The Voyage of the Dawn Treader* (Macmillan, 1952. Paper, Collier/Macmillan); *The Silver Chair* (Macmillan, 1953. Paper, Collier/Macmillan); *The Horse and His Boy* (Macmillan, 1954. Paper, Collier/Macmillan); *The Magician's Nephew,* which tells how Aslan created Narnia (Macmillan, 1955. Paper, Collier/Macmillan); and *The Last Battle* (Macmillan, 1956. Paper, Collier/Macmillan). (B-C)

The Little Prince, written and illus. by Antoine de Saint Exupéry. Harcourt, 1943. Paper, Harcourt. An aviator whose plane is forced down in the Sahara Desert encounters a little man from a small planet who describes his adventures in the universe seeking the secret of what is really important in life. (C-D)

Many Moons, by James Thurber; illus. by Louis Slobodkin. Harcourt, 1943. Paper, Harcourt/Voyager. When the spoiled little princess is determined to have the moon, the King's court is thrown into an uproar. Amply illustrated with delicate, watercolor drawings. Other fantasies for young children by this writer are *The Great Quillow* (Harcourt, 1944. Paper, Harcourt/Voyager) *The Thirteen Clocks* (Simon, 1950. Paper, Simon/Fireside); and *The Wonderful O* (Simon, 1951. Paper, Simon/Fireside). (A-B)

The Mouse and his Child, by Russell Hoban; illus. by Lillian Hoban. Harper, 1967. Paper, Avon/Camelot. The adventures of a tin father mouse and his son in their search for a magnificent dollhouse, a plush elephant, and a tin seal they had known in the toyshop. (B)

Over Sea, Under Stone, by Susan Cooper. Harcourt, 1966. Paper, Harcourt/Voyager. Set in present-day Cornwall, this fantasy is based on the legend of the grail. The first in a series of five, it portrays the involvement of three children and their parents in a struggle between the forces of good and evil. The other titles are: *The Dark Is Rising* (A Margaret K. McElderry Book/Atheneum, 1973. Paper, Atheneum/Aladdin); *Greenwitch* (A Margaret K. McElderry Book/Atheneum, 1974. Paper, Atheneum/Aladdin); *The Grey King* (A Margaret K. McElderry Book/Atheneum, 1975. Paper, Atheneum/Aladdin); and *Silver on the Tree* (A Margaret K. McElderry Book/Atheneum, 1977. Paper, Atheneum/Aladdin). (C-D)

Peter Pan, by James M. Barrie; illus. by Nora S. Unwin. Scribner, 1950. Paper, Penguin/Puffin. Wendy and her brothers have many exciting adventures in Never-Never Land with Peter Pan, the boy who never grew up. An attractive edition of a perennial favorite. (B-C)

The Phantom Tollbooth, by Norton Juster, illus. by Jules Feiffer. Random, 1961. Paper, Random. Milo, a little boy who didn't know what to do with himself, goes through the phantom tollbooth behind which lies a strange land and even stranger adventures. (B-C)

The Princess and the Goblin, by George MacDonald; illus. by Nora Unwin. Macmillan, 1951. Paper, Penguin/Puffin. In true fairy-tale fashion Curdie, the miner's son, helps Princess Irene defeat the goblins who threaten her mountain kingdom. (B)

Rabbit Hill, written and illus. by Robert Lawson. Viking, 1944. Paper, Penguin/Puffin. When "new folks" move into the house on the hill, the community animals already in residence are eager to learn whether they will be friends or enemies. This account of the doings of Little Georgie, the rabbit, his family, and friend is full of chuckles and sage observations. Its sequel is *The Tough Winter* (Viking, 1954. Paper, Penguin/Puffin). (B)

The Rescuers, by Margery Sharp and illus. by Garth Williams. Little, 1959. Paper, Dell/Yearling. Three courageous mice rescue a Norwegian poet held captive in a barbarous country. A delightful, heroic tale which will appeal to child and adult alike. Followed by *Miss Bianca* (Little, 1962. Paper, Dell/Yearling). (B-C)

A String in the Harp, by Nancy Bond. A Margaret McElderry Book/ Atheneum, 1967. Young Peter Morgan is magically drawn into past events in Wales when he finds the lost harp key of Taliesin. His strange adventures help him to cope and accept his family situation as it exists in the world of the present. (C-D)

Tom's Midnight Garden, by Philippa Pearce; illus. by Susan Einzig. Lippincott, 1959. Paper, Dell/Yearling. Tom's dull holiday becomes exciting when the clock strikes thirteen, enabling him to go back into the past. An unusual theme handled with perception. (B-C)

Tuck Everlasting, written and illus. by Natalie Babbitt. Farrar, 1975. Paper, Bantam. Life without death is not without problems for the Tuck family. A provocative and novel look at the natural sequence of living. (C)

The Wind Eye, by Robert Westall. Greenwillow, 1977. A small boat used in St. Cuthbert's time for conveying the dead is the vehicle for the time-travel adventures of a contemporary English family. A compelling tale. (C-D)

Science Fiction

Alice, by Kirill Bulychev; tr. by Mirra Ginsburg. Macmillan, 1977. Some incidents in the life of a little girl of the twenty-first century, recorded by her father on the eve of her first day in school. (B)

Children of Morrow, by H. M. Hoover. Four Winds, 1973. Beaten and abused in their communal home, two extraordinary children use their strange gifts for running away to happiness. Followed by *Treasures of Morrow* (Four Winds, 1976). (C)

Crusade in Jeans, by Thea Beckman. Scribner, 1976. The heartbreaking, thirteenth-century Children's Crusade as experienced by stranded modern-time traveler Dolf. (C-D)

Forgotten Door, by Alexander Key. Westminster, 1965. Paper, Scholastic. Amnesiac Jon can only remember falling through a door onto Earth where his strange and wonderful talents give rise to both awe and danger. (B-C)

Have Space Suit, Will Travel, by Robert Heinlein. Scribner, 1958. Paper, Ballantine. College-bound Kip tries out his contest space suit and attracts combatants in an interspatial war. (B-C)

Is There Life on a Plastic Planet? by Mildred Ames. Dutton, 1975. Could a life-sized talking doll change places with Hollis, and even fool her parents? (B-C)

Miss Pickerell Goes to Mars, by Ellen MacGregor. McGraw, 1951. Miss Pickerell is protesting the presence of a spaceship in her pasture when she is unexpectedly carried off to Mars. This is one of a series that will appeal to young listeners. (B)

Mrs. Frisby and the Rats of NIMH, by Robert C. O'Brien; illus. by Zena Bernstein. Atheneum, 1971. Paper, Atheneum/Aladdin. Mrs. Frisby is motivated by mouse motherhood when she asks the runaway reading rats of NIMH for help. Also by the same author: *The Silver Crown* (Atheneum, 1968. Paper, Atheneum/Aladdin) and *Z for Zachariah* (Atheneum, 1974. Paper, Dell). (B-C)

The Science Fiction Bestiary: Nine Stories of Science Fiction, ed. by

Robert Silverberg. Nelson, 1971. Paper, Dell. Tales of fantastic science-fiction fauna selected from the files of old magazines. (C-D)

Space Ship under the Apple Tree, by Louis Slobodkin. Macmillan, 1952. Paper, Collier/Macmillan. Eddie finds Marty, the spaceman from Martinea, standing upside down in the apple tree near his astral rocket disk. This is the first in a series which has appeal for the younger child. (B)

This Star Shall Abide, by Sylvia L. Engdahl, drawings by Richard Cuffari. Atheneum, 1972. Paper, Atheneum/Aladdin. Noren is declared an outlaw heretic when he challenges the custodial right of the Scholars and their servant Technicians to all his planet's knowledge. Followed by *Beyond the Tomorrow Mountains,* (Atheneum, 1973). (C-D)

The Turning Place: Stories of a Future Past, by Jean E. Karl. Dutton, 1976. Paper, Dell/Yearling. Nine intriguing stories contrasting and combining realistic characters with imaginative situations. Another book by this writer, but for younger children, is *Beloved, Benjamin Is Waiting* (Dutton, 1978. Paper, Dell/Yearling), in which Lucinda seeks shelter in an abandoned house in a cemetery where she finds an effigy which speaks to her. (C-D)

Twenty-One Balloons, written and illus. by William Pène du Bois. Viking, 1947. Paper, Dell/Yearling. Professor William Waterman Sherman leaves San Francisco on August 15, 1883, in a balloon, with the intention of flying across the Pacific Ocean. (B-C)

Twenty Thousand Leagues under the Sea, by Jules Verne. Dodd, 1952. Paper, Airmont. An imaginative Frenchman writes of Captain Nemo and his fantastic adventures with a submarine in the 1860s. This author's *From the Earth to the Moon* (Paper, Scholastic) relates the strange adventures of three nineteenth-century astronauts shot to the moon by an enormous gun. (C-D)

The Visitors, by John Rowe Townsend. Lippincott, 1977. Tourists are expected during June in Cambridge, but John Dunham suspects the Wyatt family of being very unusual travelers. (C)

The Weathermonger, by Peter Dickinson. Atlantic/Little, 1969. Paper, DAW Books/New American Library. Geoffrey, the weathermonger, and his sister, Sally, search for the source of the mysterious changes which have returned the British Isles to medieval superstition and fear. (C)

The White Mountains, by John Christopher. Macmillan, 1967. Paper, Collier/Macmillan. Three boys flee to promised safety in the Alps in a future world where all fourteen-year-olds are robbed of independent thought by steel caps the Tripod implanted in their skulls. Followed by *The City of Gold and Lead* (Macmillan, 1967. Paper, Collier/Macmillan) and *The Pool of Fire* (Macmillan, 1968. Paper, Collier/Macmillan). (B-C)

The Wonderful Flight to the Mushroom Planet, by Eleanor Cameron; illus. by Robert Henneberger. Atlantic/Little, 1954. Paper, Scholastic. David and Chuck build a spaceship and journey to the unknown planet of Basidium. There are other "Mushroom Planet" stories, all of which are enjoyed by younger children. (B)

A Wrinkle in Time, by Madeleine L'Engle. Farrar, 1962. Paper, Dell/Yearling. Precocious Charles Wallace and his sister Meg use a tesseract to rescue their imprisoned father. And, in *A Wind in the Door* (Farrar, 1973. Paper, Dell/Yearling), Meg plays an important part in Charles's struggle between life and death. (C)

ZOO 2000: Twelve Stories of Science Fiction and Fantasy Beasts, comp. by Jane Yolen. Houghton/Clarion, 1973. Animals of the sci-fi future, where even the ordinary is fabulous. (C-D)

People and Places

Abe Lincoln Grows Up, by Carl Sandburg; illus. by James Daugherty. Harcourt, 1928. Paper, Harcourt/Voyager. The first twenty-seven chapters of the author's classic, *Abraham Lincoln: The Prairie Years,* are retold in simple, poetic style, with emphasis on Lincoln's boyhood. (B-C)

Amos Fortune, Free Man, by Elizabeth Yates; illus. by Nora S. Unwin.

Dutton, 1950. Paper, Dell/Yearling. Taken captive and brought to America from his native Africa where he was a prince, Amos Fortune bought his own freedom and that of several other persons. This is a sensitive and moving story of a man who loved God and his fellow men. (B-C)

Anne Frank: The Diary of a Young Girl, by Anne Frank. Doubleday, 1967. Paper, Pocket Books. The candid thoughts of an adolescent who hid for two years from the Nazis in an Amsterdam office building. (C-D)

Behind the Sealed Door, by Irene and Laurence Swinburne. Sniffen Court/Atheneum, 1977. An account of the discovery of the tomb and treasures of Tutankhamun, copiously illustrated with photographs, many in color. (B-C)

Carry On, Mr. Bowditch, by Jean Lee Latham; illus. by John O. Cosgrave II. Houghton, 1955. Paper, Houghton/Sandpiper. A boy who was "quick at figures" learned all he could about ships and the sea, as well as about mathematics and astronomy, and became a famous navigator. (C)

A Child in Prison Camp, by Takashima. Morrow, 1974. A Japanese-Canadian artist recreates her family's experiences in an internment camp during World War II. With watercolor illustrations by the author. (C)

A Day of Pleasure: Stories of a Boy Growing Up in Warsaw, by Isaac Bashevis Singer. Farrar, 1969. Paper, Farrar. Nineteen autobiographical stories about childhood in Poland from 1908 to 1918. Illustrated with photos. (C-D)

The Endless Steppe: Growing Up in Siberia, by Esther Hautzig. Crowell, 1968. Paper, Scholastic. The author relates her experiences during a five-year stay in Siberia with her family during World War II, after they were arrested as political enemies. (C-D)

The Girl with Spunk, by Judith St. George. Putnam, 1975. A memorable recreation of a girl's struggles against the attitudes of the times. Deals with women's rights in New York State during the 1840s. (C)

Grandmother's Pictures, by Sam Cornish; illus. by Jeanne John. Brad-

bury, 1976. Paper, Bookstore Pr.   Mysterious and somewhat precocious ancestor stories form a young boy's remembrances of his
grandmother, her room, her possessions, and old photographs.   (B)

Harriet Tubman, Conductor on the Underground Railroad, by Ann
Petry. Crowell, 1955. Paper, Archway.   A brave and ingenious
woman, who escapes slavery via the Underground Railroad, leads
several hundred others to freedom.   (C)

The Helen Keller Story, by Catherine O. Peare. Crowell, 1959.   This is
a dramatic account of a remarkable woman's progress in overcom-
ing deafness, muteness, and blindness.   (B-C)

In Their Own Words: A History of the American Negro, 1619-1865, ed.
by Milton Meltzer. Crowell, 1964. Paper, Apollo.   First in a series
which relates the history of American blacks through their own
writings. It includes excerpts from books, letters, documents, and
the like. Other volumes cover the periods from 1865 to 1916 and
1916 to 1966.   (C-D)

Kon Tiki, by Thor Heyerdahl. Rand, 1950. Paper, Ballantine.   Six men
cross 4000 miles of South Pacific ocean on a balsa-log raft. A modern classic of survival.   (C-D)

Lumberjack, by William Kurelek. Houghton, 1974.   Life in various
Canadian lumber camps is depicted through twenty-six paintings
by this Canadian artist. He also shows the Nativity scene against the
background of the northern prairies in *A Northern Nativity: Christmas Dreams of a Prairie Boy.* (Tundra, 1976).   (B-C)

Many Smokes, Many Moons, by Jamake Highwater. Lippincott,
1978.   A chronology of American Indian history through Indian
art.   (C-D)

Martin Luther King: The Peaceful Warrior, 3rd ed., by Ed Clayton; illus. by David Hodges. Prentice, 1968. Paper, Archway.   One of the
most readable biographies for younger children, this includes
the words and music for "We Shall Overcome."   (B)

Me and Willie and Pa: The Story of Abraham Lincoln and His Son Tad,
by F. N. Monjo; illus. by Douglas Gorsline. Simon, 1973.   A touch-
ing story about Lincoln and his family written in the unsophisti-

cated manner of a young child. *The Drinking Gourd* (Harper, 1969), also by Monjo, presents a real Underground Railroad incident. (B)

Mischling, Second Degree: My Childhood in Nazi Germany, by Ilse Koehn. Greenwillow, 1977. Paper, Bantam. Because having one Jewish grandparent gives Ilse a precarious position in Hitler's Germany, her loving parents divorce to protect her. A moving narrative of growing up in Berlin and in a Nazi youth camp in Czechoslovakia. (C-D)

Never to Forget: The Jews of the Holocaust, by Milton Meltzer. Harper, 1976. Paper, Dell/Yearling. A grim account of individuals and events involved in this twentieth-century example of moral indifference and man's inhumanity to man. (D)

On the Frontier with Mr. Audubon, by Barbara Brenner. Coward, 1977. Through the fictionalized journal of a young apprentice, one learns and understands how precisely this artist approached his work. Illustrated with examples of Audubon's work. (B)

Paddle-to-the-Sea, written and illus. by Holling C. Holling. Houghton, 1941. Large, full-page illustrations in color help tell the experiences of a little carved Indian as he journeys in his canoe through the Great Lakes and down the St. Lawrence River to the sea. (B)

Pyramid, by David Macaulay. Houghton, 1975. Detailed drawings and clear text describe the construction of a pyramid from site selection to burial. (C)

The Silver Crest: My Russian Boyhood, by Kornei Chukovsky. Holt, 1976. The Russian poet, in a translation by Beatrice Stillman, uses a light touch in presenting a glimpse of his beloved Odessa at the turn of the century, and the problems of class discrimination, poverty, and corruption which affected his future. (C-D)

The Tall Man from Boston, by Marion L. Starkey; illus. by Charles Mikolaycak. Crown, 1975. A simple account of the events in Salem Village focusing on John Alden, unjustly accused of witchcraft. (B-C)

To Be a Slave, by Julius Lester; illus. by Tom Feelings. Dial, 1968. Paper, Dell/Yearling. The history of slavery is told in the words of the slaves themselves. The sympathetic commentary and the graphic illustrations combine to make a powerful book for children and adults.   (D)

Voyaging to Cathay: America in the China Trade, by Alfred Tamarin and Shirley Glubok. Viking, 1976.   A beautifully designed book about America's nineteenth-century trade with China, with illustrations selected from objects, engravings, and photographs relating to the period.   (B-C)

What's the Big Idea, Ben Franklin? by Jean Fritz; illus. by Margot Tomes. Coward, 1976.   A historically accurate, irreverent look at our famous forefather.   (B-C)

The Writings of W. E. B. DuBois, ed. by Virginia Hamilton. Crowell, 1975.   The life and thoughts, as well as the times, of the distinguished black scholar and activist are presented in this well-edited book.   (D)

The Arts

The Art of Africa, by Shirley Glubok; special photography by Alfred H. Tamarin. Harper, 1965.   Striking photographs and brief text introduce the varying styles and forms of art found in many areas and tribes of Africa. Similar volumes by this author cover other countries and cultures.   (B-C)

The Art of Photography, by Shirley Glubok; designed by Gerard Nook. Macmillan, 1977.   A satisfying blend of information and photographs unfolds the history of a century-old art.   (C)

The Arts of Wood, by Christine Price. Scribner, 1976.   Household items from all over the world are considered both as art and as examples of the life-style of people from diverse cultures. Detailed illustrations by the author add to the interest of this volume.   (B-C)

Books: From Writer to Reader, by Howard Greenfield. Crown, 1976. Paper, Crown. Every step involved in producing books is described in lucid text and appropriate illustrations. A well-designed book for both the child and the adult. (C-D)

Castle, written and illus. by David Macaulay. Houghton, 1977. Text and detailed black-and-white drawings follow the planning and construction of a typical fortified castle and adjoining walled town in thirteenth-century Wales. Companion volumes are *Cathedral: The Story of Its Construction* (Houghton, 1973); *City: A Story of Roman Planning and Construction* (Houghton, 1974); and *Underground* (Houghton, 1976). (C-D)

Chinese Writing: An Introduction, by Diane Wolff; calligraphy by Jeanette Chien. Holt, 1975. An introduction to the characteristics of written and spoken Chinese with a discussion of calligraphy and instructions for writing characters. (C)

Colonial Craftsmen: The Beginnings of American Industry, written and illus. by Edwin Tunis. Crowell, 1976. Comprehensive and detailed, this describes how the occupations of skilled tradespeople and professional artisans developed from handcrafts to American industries. *Colonial Living* (Crowell, 1957) describes, in the same minute detail, life in the thirteen colonies. (C-D)

Contemporary American Folk Artists, by Elinor L. Horwitz and J. Roderick Moore. Lippincott, 1975. Paper, Lippincott. The strangely moving creations of untutored people who paint, whittle, and build bizarre environments to fulfill a need within themselves. Illustrated with photographs. A companion volume, by Horwitz, is *Mountain People, Mountain Crafts* (Lippincott, 1974. Paper, Lippincott). (C-D)

Dancing Masks of Africa, by Christine Price. Scribner, 1973. A rhythmic story of the powerful ceremonial masks of the West African people and the prominent part these masks play in their daily life. (B-C)

The Heritage Sampler: A Book of Colonial Arts and Crafts, by Cheryl G. Hoople; pictures by Richard Cuffari. Dial, 1975. This volume discusses the practical necessity of the crafts employed by the American colonists and includes instructions for duplicating those crafts today. (B-C)

An Introduction to Shakespeare, by Marchette Chute. Dutton, 1951. The excitement of Shakespeare's theater is vividly brought to life with detailed information on how the plays were written, costumed, and presented.   (D)

Latin American Crafts and Their Cultural Backgrounds, By Jeremy Comins. Lothrop, 1974.   Here are instructions for making sculpture, jewelry, and other objects in the style of ancient and modern Latin American craftsmen.   (C)

Letters to Horseface: Being the Story of Wolfgang Amadeus Mozart's Journey to Italy, 1769-1770, When He Was a Boy of Fourteen, by F. N. Monjo; illus. by Don Bolognese and Elaine Raphael. Viking, 1975.   These imaginary letters, based on fact, from Mozart to his sister Nannerl describe his trip through Italy with his father.   (B-C)

Looking at Architecture, by Roberta M. Paine. Lothrop, 1974.   A short, readable history of architecture which examines some of the great buildings of the world, from the Egyptian pyramids to modern skyscrapers.   (B-C)

Making Things: The Hand Book of Creative Discoveries, by Ann Wiseman. 2 vols., Little, 1975. Paper, Little.   Instructions for making over a hundred items from paper, potatoes, leaves, rope, bread, clay, and other easily available materials are provided in these useful volumes.(B-C)

The Meaning of Music: The Young Listener's Guide, by Jean Seligmann and Juliet Danziger. Philomel, 1966.   An unusually fine introduction to music, its language, forms, and composers that includes as well descriptions of the instruments found in a symphony orchestra.   (C-D)

Paint, Brush, and Palette, by Harvey Weiss. Addison, 1966.   This describes for the beginner some of the basic techniques of painting. The author's *Paper, Ink, and Roller: Print-Making for Beginners* (Addison, 1958) is another book on basic techniques.   (B-C)

The Pantheon Story of Art for Young People, rev. ed., by Ariane Ruskin Batterberry. Pantheon, 1975.   This work explores man's creative talents, from cave painting to modern abstracts, with emphasis on major works and artists of each period. Included are many full-page reproductions in color.   (C-D)

Pieter Brueghel's The Fair, story by Ruth Craft. Lippincott, 1975. Vigorous original verses accompany various portions from the Brueghel painting, all reproduced in full color. The result is an experiencing and sharing of all the events of the fair. (B-C)

Simple Printmaking, by Peter Weiss; illus. by Sally Gralla. Lothrop, 1976. For beginners, this is a simple and attractive guide to making prints from objects or materials from nature. Printing with rollers and stencils, marbling, and printing on fabric are included. (B)

Tales from Shakespeare, rev. ed., by Charles and Mary Lamb; illus. by Richard M. Powers. Macmillan, 1963. Paper, Dutton. The Lambs still provide for younger children the best introduction to these classics. *Stories from Shakespeare,* by Marchette Chute (Philomel, 1956. Paper, New American Library), is an excellent retelling for older children. (C)

A Very Young Dancer, by Jill Krementz. Knopf, 1976. A ten-year-old student at the School of American Ballet in New York describes her classes and the preparation for and performance of her role in the New York City Ballet's production of "The Nutcracker." Lavishly illustrated with excellent photographs. (B)

The Wonderful World of Nature and Science

About Owls, by May Garelick; illus. by Tony Chen. Four Winds, 1975. A handsome picture book focusing on the Elf Owl, the Barn Owl, and the Great Horned Owl. (A)

The Amazing Dandelion, by Millicent E. Selsam. Morrow, 1977. The familiar dandelion is examined as to its uses, why it spreads so rapidly, and why it is so hardy. With outstanding photographs by Jerome Wexler. (B)

Animals and Their Niches: How Species Share Resources. by

Laurence Pringle; illus. by Leslie Morrill. Morrow, 1977.   Based on research, this book provides insight into the fascinating ways in which animals coexist in woods, fields, and ponds.   (B)

Aquarium Book for Boys and Girls, rev. ed., by Alfred P. Morgan. Scribner, 1959.   Clear, definite, interesting information is given on the care and housing of frogs, goldfish, toads, turtles, and other inhabitants of the aquarium.   (B-C)

The Bat, by Nina Leen. Holt, 1976.   An intimate look at the daily life of the bat that is copiously illustrated with striking photographs. (B)

Birds and Their Nests, new ed., by Gwynne Vevers. McGraw, 1973. Both common and unusual birds—in trees, on the ground, on water—are well described. Includes excellent illustrations by Colin Threadgall.   (B)

The Blossom on the Bough: A Book of Trees, by Anne Ophelia Dowden. Crowell, 1975.   Many illustrations, some in full color, expand the descriptions of regional trees and their blossoms. For the young botanist. Well-indexed.   (C-D)

A Chick Hatches, by Joanna Cole. Morrow, 1976.   The simple text and the excellent photographs of Jerome Wexler describe the development of a chicken from the appearance of the first white spot on the yolk to the fluffy bird that hatches.   (A)

The Cloud Book, by Tomie de Paola. Holiday, 1975. Paper, Scholastic.   Introduces the ten most common types of clouds, the myths that have been inspired by their shapes, and what they can tell about coming weather changes. A companion informational picture book is *The Quicksand Book* (Holiday, 1977).   (A)

Death Is Natural, by Laurence Pringle. Four Winds, 1977.   Using the example of a rabbit killed by a car, the author explores in simple, clear language the role of plants and animals in maintaining the delicate ecobalance of nature.   (C)

Discovering the American Stork, by Jack Denton Scott; photographs by Ozzie Sweet. Harcourt, 1976.   A photographic essay on this fascinating bird.   (C)

A Dog's Books of Birds, by Peter Parnall. Scribner, 1977. A curious dog explores bird life while the listener accumulates bits of information about birds and has a good time, too! (A-B)

Elephants, by Joe Van Wormer. Dutton, 1976. Text and photographs introduce the characteristics and habits of Asian and African elephants. (B)

Fish and How They Reproduce, by Dorothy Hinshaw Patent. Holiday, 1976. Characteristics of fish, their reproductive habits, and their means of survival are clearly and interestingly presented. Excellent black-and-white drawings by Matthew Kalmenoff clarify the text. Another fine science book by this writer is *Evolution Goes on Every Day* (Holiday, 1976). (B-C)

Grizzly Bear, by Berniece Freschet; illus. by Donald Carrick. Scribner, 1975. A handsome book portraying a year in the life of a grizzly and her cubs in a format young children will enjoy. (A)

The Harlequin Moth: Its Life Story, by Millicent E. Selsam. Morrow, 1975. Fine photographs by Jerome Wexler and a brief text illuminate the life cycle of this beautiful moth. (B)

He and She: How Males and Females Behave, by S. Carl Hirsch; illus. by William Steinel. Lippincott, 1975. Findings of ethologists regarding male/female relationships, both instinctive and cultural, are presented. (C)

Houses from the Sea, by Alice E. Goudey; illus. by Adrienne Adams. Scribner, 1959. Paper, Scribner. A beautifully illustrated and scientifically accurate picture book on sea shells. In rhythmic prose the author tells of two children who spend a day at the beach collecting shells. (A)

How Did We Find Out about Outer Space? by Isaac Asimov; illus. by David Wool. Walker, 1977. The history of flying from the legend of Daedalus to the rockets of Goddard and von Braun will whet the appetite for further material on space. (B-C)

How to Be a Nature Detective, by Millicent Selsam; illus. by Ezra Jack Keats. Harper, 1963. An easy-to-read book that will help children identify such varying clues of nature as animal tracks and bits of hair. (A)

How to Count Like a Martian, by Glory St. John. Walck, 1975. An attractively illustrated account of how Egyptians and other ancient people counted, and how they recorded their numbers. Counting on the abacus and the computer are also described. (B-C)

The I Hate Mathematics! Book, by Marilyn Burns; illus. by Martha Hairston. A Brown Paper School Book/Little, 1975. Paper, Little. Delightful collection of puzzles about topology, logic, geometry, primes, clock arithmetic, and more. (B-C)

Introducing Archaeology, by Magnus Magnusson; illus. by Martin Simmons. Walck, 1972. Paper, Walck. Discusses the development of archaeology as a science and its role in reconstructing history. (D)

Life Story, written and illus. by Virginia Lee Burton. Houghton, 1962. Paper, Houghton. Striking paintings and sketches with brief text depict the evolution of the earth and living things as a continuously developing drama. (B-C)

Listen to the Crow, by Laurence Pringle; illus. by Ted Lewin. Crowell, 1976. The language of the crow and its possible meaning, the legends, and this bird's adaptation to the human world are discussed in this attractively illustrated book. (B-C)

Look to the Night Sky: An Introduction to Sky Watching, by Seymour Simon. Viking, 1977. Paper, Penguin/Puffin. Directed to beginners, this introduces them to observing planets, comets and meteors, and other celestial events. Also included is advice on buying and using telescopes. (C)

Peeper, First Voice of Spring, by Robert M. McClung; illus. by Carol Lerner. Morrow, 1977. An account of the tree frog's life cycle, beautifully written and illustrated. (A-B)

Skunk for a Day, by Roger Caras; illus. by Diane Paterson. Windmill, 1976. Follows the activities of a young skunk from nightfall till dawn as he forages for food. *Coyote for a Day* (Windmill, 1977) is another simple book dealing with the life activities of a much maligned species. (B)

Small Worlds Close Up, by Lisa Grillone and Joseph Gennaro. Crown,

1978. Fascinating photographs of things animal, vegetable, and mineral as seen through an electron microscope. (B-D)

Terrariums, by John Hoke. Watts, 1972. Each construction step is clearly outlined in text and illustration. (B-C)

Think Metric! by Franklyn M. Branley; illus. by Graham Booth. Crowell, 1973. The history, practical uses, and the reasons for changing to this system are put simply in terms meaningful to children. (B)

The View from the Oak: The Private World of Other Creatures, by Judith Kohl and Herbert Kohl. Sierra Club/Scribner. 1977. Paper, Scribner. Encourages the reader to perceive the world as a wide range of animals does by including games, activities, and related experiments designed to help the reader enter these different worlds through an understanding of the senses of the animals themselves. (C-D)

What Makes Day and Night, by Franklyn M. Branley; illus. by Helen Borten. Crowell, 1961. Paper, Crowell/Crocodile. A science picture book which explains, for young children, how the turning of the earth causes night and day. (A-B)

Wildflowers and the Stories Behind Their Names, by Phyllis S. Busch. Scribner, 1977. Anne Ophelia Dowden's extraordinary actual-size illustrations, in color and black and white, accompany the brief descriptions of the plants included in this volume. Although not a field guide, it will lead the user into plant identification, plant lore, and other interesting information. (C-D)

Window into a Nest, by Geraldine Lux Flanagan and Sean Morris. Houghton, 1976. In the form of a diary, the book suggests ways to study animal behavior close to home. (B)

Wrapped for Eternity: The Story of the Egyptian Mummies, by Mildred M. Pace; line drawings by Tom Huffman. McGraw, 1974. Paper, Dell. Explores the mysteries of the mummification process, tomb robbing, x-raying of mummy bundles, and myths about mummies. (B-C)

Rhymes and Poetry

Amelia Mixed the Mustard and Other Poems, comp. by Evaline Ness. Scribner, 1975.   An attractive selection of lively poems and nonsense verses which show the individuality of females.   (A-B)

America Is Not All Traffic Lights: Poems of the Midwest, by Alice Fleming. Little, 1976.   A slim, attractive volume which provides the flavor of the rural Midwest through works of its poets. Illustrated with photographs.   (C)

Bronzeville Boys and Girls, by Gwendolyn Brooks; illus. by Ronni Solbert. Harper, 1956.   Simple and perceptive verses written by the well-known black poet and Pulitzer Prize winner.   (B-C)

Cats and Bats and Things with Wings: Poems, by Conrad Aiken; illus. by Milton Glaser. Atheneum, 1965.   Sixteen poems about strange and familiar animals are excellent for reading aloud. Striking illustrations.   (B-C)

A Child's Garden of Verses, by Robert Louis Stevenson; illus. by Erik Blegvad. Random, 1978.   A picture-book version of the favorite poems.   (A-B)

Come Hither, new ed., col. by Walter de la Mare; illus. by Warren Chappell. Knopf, 1957.   A famous English poet has collected nearly five hundred poems "for the young of all ages" and provided notes of special interest.   (B-C)

Coplas: Folk Poems in Spanish and English, ed. by Toby Talbot; illus. by Rocco Negri. Four Winds, 1972.   A distinctive bilingual collection of folk poems that orginated in Spain and that were brought to the "New World" by the conquistadors.   (D)

Favorite Poems, Old and New, ed. by Helen Ferris; illus. by Leonard Weisgard. Doubleday, 1957.   A fat, generous volume of favorite rhymes and verses.   (B-C)

Free to Be . . . You and Me, conceived by Marlo Thomas; ed. by Carol Hart, Letty Cottin Pogrebin, and Mary Rodgers. McGraw, 1974.

Paper, McGraw. Songs, stories, and poems which encourage freedom from traditional or stereotyped sex roles. Originally produced as a TV special. (B-D)

The Golden Journey: Poems for Young People, comp. by Louise Bogan and William Jay Smith; illus. by Fritz Kredel. Paper, Contemporary, 1976. This imaginative assortment ranges from Shakespeare to Dylan Thomas. Stylized woodcuts introduce nineteen subject areas in this distinguished collection. (C-D)

Golden Slippers: An Anthology of Negro Poetry for Young Readers, comp. by Arna Bontemps. Harper, 1941. This collection recognizes the significant contributions of such outstanding poets as Langston Hughes, James Weldon Johnson, Countee Cullen, and Paul Lawrence Dunbar. (B-C)

A Great Big Ugly Man Came Up and Tied His Horse To Me: A Book of Nonsense Verse, comp. and illus. by Wallace Tripp. Little, 1973. Paper, Little. A collection of classic nonsense verse made even funnier by Tripp's uninhibited animals. (A-B)

I Met a Man, by John Ciardi; illus. by Robert Osborn. Houghton, 1961. Paper, Houghton/Sandpiper. Riddles, jokes, and humor, all in rhyme, and all written by this poet for his daughter's first reading experience. (A-B)

In a Spring Garden, ed. by Richard Lewis; illus. by Ezra Jack Keats. Dial, 1965. Paper, Dial/Pied Piper. Twenty-four haiku poems reflect a beautiful spring day in text and in illustration. (A)

In the Trail of the Wind: American Indian Poems and Ritual Orations, ed. by John Bierhorst. Farrar, 1971. Paper, Farrar. Poems, chants, war songs, and incantations of ancient and modern Indians of North America. (C-D)

Let's Marry Said the Cherry, and Other Nonsense Rhymes, written and illus. by N. M. Bodecker. A Margaret K. McElderry Book/Atheneum, 1974. Paper, Atheneum/Aladdin. Hilarious drawings extend the delightful nonsense of the rhymes. (A)

Miracles: Poems by Children of the English Speaking World, comp. by Richard Lewis. Simon, 1966. Poems chosen with a keen appreciation of the spontaneity of children's creative expression. (C)

More Cricket Songs: Japanese Haiku, trans. by Harry Behn. Harcourt, 1971.   A companion volume to *Cricket Songs* (Harcourt, 1964) in which haiku verses are complemented with paintings by Japanese masters.   (B)

Nightmares: Poems to Trouble Your Sleep. by Jack Prelutsky; illus. by Arnold Lobel. Greenwillow, 1976.   "Poems to trouble your sleep" with properly terrifying full-page illustrations!   (B-C)

Oh, How Silly! sel. by William Cole; illus. by Tomi Ungerer. Viking, 1970.   Fifty-five humorous poems by English and American poets with clever line drawings.   (B-C)

Reflections on a Gift of Watermelon Pickle . . . and Other Modern Verse, comp. by Stephen Dunning, Edward Lueders, and Hugh Smith. Lothrop, 1966.   A fine collection of modern verse superbly illustrated with photographs, a combination that will appeal to older children.   (D)

Season Songs, by Ted Hughes; pictures by Leonard Baskin. Viking, 1975.   A beautiful and powerful volume, both in terms of the verses and the watercolors and drawings which accompany them. Will appeal to both the child and the adult.   (B-C)

Small Poems, by Valerie Worth; pictures by Natalie Babbitt. Farrar, 1972.   Familiar things in a child's life—porch, chair, dog, pie, and grass—described in verse.   (A-B)

Spin a Soft Black Song: Poems for Children, by Nikki Giovanni; illus. by Charles Bible. Hill, 1971.   Poems written for black children but which speak to everyone in this picture book.   (A-B)

This Way Delight: A Book of Poetry for the Young, ed. by Herbert Read; illus. by Juliet Kepes. Pantheon, 1956.   Poems that appeal to the imagination are emphasized in this unusually attractive anthology. Includes works of well-known poets as well as those of newer, more recent poets.   (C-D)

When We Were Very Young, rev. ed., by A. A. Milne; illus. by E. H. Shepard. Dutton, 1961. Paper, Dell/Yearling.   These verses, written for and about a small boy of his real and make-believe world, are now a modern classic as are the inimitable illustrations. A companion volume is *Now We Are Six* (rev. ed., Dutton, 1961. Paper,

Dell/Yearling). *The World of Christopher Robin* (Dutton, 1958) combines the two books in one volume.   (A-B)

Who Look at Me, by June Jordan. Crowell, 1969.   Reproductions of paintings which reflect the experience of black people in America from slavery days to the present, accompanied by lines from a modern interpretative poem.   (C-D)

Celebrations

Autumn

Ghosts and Goblins, rev. ed., by Wilhelmina Harper; illus. by William Wiesner. Dutton, 1965.   Good stories of strange and mysterious happenings, spooky enough for Halloween, are fun for telling or reading aloud at any time of the year.   (B)

Hard Scrabble Harvest, written and illus. by Dahlov Ipcar. Doubleday, 1976.   A picture book, in rhyme, which relates the struggle of the farmer against the odds from spring planting to fall harvest and Thanksgiving dinner.   (A)

The House on the Roof: A Sukkot Story, by David A. Adler; illus. by Marilyn Hirsh. Bonim, 1976.   When an old man builds a Sukkah hut on the roof of his apartment building, the owner of the building takes him to court.   (A-B)

The Jewish New Year, by Molly Cone; illus. by Jerome Snyder. Crowell, 1966.   This picture book explains to the young child the meaning of Rosh Hashanah and Yom Kippur, the Jewish New Year holidays.   (A-B)

The Mice Came in Early This Year, by Eleanor J. Lapp; illus. by David Cunningham. Whitman, 1976.   A child observes the preparations made by his family and by the wild creatures outdoors as autumn approaches.   (A)

Winter

Amahl and the Night Visitors, by Gian-Carlo Menotti; illus. by Roger Duvoisin. McGraw, 1952. Adapted by Frances Frost from the contemporary opera by the same name, this is the story of a crippled boy and his mother whose poor home sheltered the Wise Men on their way to Bethlehem. (B-C)

Baboushka and the Three Kings, ad. by Ruth Robbins; illus. by Nicholas Sidjakov. Parnassus, 1960. A beautifully illustrated edition of the Russian folktale of the old woman who missed her chance to travel with the three Kings and who has been searching for the Christ Child ever since. (A-B)

A Certain Small Shepherd, by Rebecca Caudill; illus. by William Pène du Bois. Holt, 1965. Paper, Holt/Owlet. Set in the mountains of Appalachia, this moving story concerns a mute boy who looks forward to being a shepherd in the Christmas pageant. Beautifully detailed illustrations. (B)

A Child's Christmas in Wales, by Dylan Thomas; woodcuts by Ellen Raskin. New Directions, 1959. Paper, New Directions. A Welsh poet recalls the celebration of Christmas in Wales and the feeling it evoked in him as a child. (C-D)

The Chinese New Year, by Cheng Hou-tien. Holt, 1976. Simple text and beautiful paper-cuts by the author describe the joys of a month-long holiday. (B)

Christmas, written and illus. by Barbara Cooney. Crowell, 1967. Ancient non-Christian winter celebrations as well as the Gospel version of the birth of Jesus are included in this simple and informative book with lovely illustrations for young children. (A)

Hanukkah Story, written and illus. by Marilyn Hirsh. Bonim, 1977. The festival of the lights is described in a simple, attractive format. (A-B)

Spring

The Boy Who Didn't Believe in Spring, by Lucille Clifton; illus. by Brinton Turkle. Dutton, 1973. Paper, Dutton/Anytime Books.   Two skeptical city boys set out to find spring which they've heard is "just around the corner." Detailed pictures in color also tell the story.   (A-B)

The Country Bunny and the Little Gold Shoes, by DuBose Heyward; illus. by Marjorie Flack. Houghton, 1939. Paper, Houghton/Sandpiper.   Drawings in pastel colors illustrate this charming tale of the little country bunny who wanted to become one of the five Easter bunnies.   (A-B)

The Egg Tree, written and illus. by Katherine Milhous. Scribner, 1950.   A sprightly picture book describes a Pennsylvania Dutch family's Easter customs—hunting for Easter eggs, decorating them, and hanging them on a traditional egg tree.   (A-B)

Hearts, Cupids, and Red Roses: The Story of the Valentine Symbols, by Edna Barth; illus. by Ursula Arndt. Houghton/Clarion, 1974. The history of Valentine's Day and the little-known stories behind its symbols. Companion volumes are *Lilies, Rabbits, and Painted Eggs: The Story of the Easter Symbols* (Houghton/Clarion, 1970) and *Shamrocks, Harps, and Shillelaghs: The Story of the St. Patrick's Day Symbols* (Houghton/Clarion, 1977).   (B-C)

Purim, by Molly Cone; illus. by Helen Borten. Crowell, 1967. One of the Crowell Holiday Books series which describes in picture-book format how Purim began and how it has been celebrated by the Jewish people throughout the ages.   (A-B)

Swamp Spring, by Carol Carrick; illus. by Donald Carrick. Macmillan, 1969.   The wonder and mystery of the season's change, when winter thaws and plants and animals awake to spring, are beautifully shown in this picture book.   (A-B)

Summer

The Fourth of July Story, by Alice Dalgliesh; illus. by Marie Nonnast. Scribner, 1956. Paper, Scribner. An account of the Continental Congress, some of its leaders, and the events which led to the framing and signing of the Declaration of Independence, simply told and colorfully illustrated for young readers. (B)

Midsummer Magic: A Garland of Stories, Charms, and Recipes, comp. by Ellin Greene; illus. by Barbara Cooney. Lothrop, 1977. A lively retelling of seven legends dealing with summer beliefs, plus fascinating bits of lore and recipes for currant cake, fruit soup, and other good things to eat. (B-C)

One Summer Night, written and illus. by Eleanor Schick. Greenwillow, 1977. Instead of going to sleep, Laura puts on a record and starts dancing and soon all her neighbors join in. An easy-to-read picture book. (A)

The Summer Maker: An Ojibway Indian Myth, ret. by Margery Bernstein and Janet Kobrin; illus. by Anne Burgess. Scribner, 1977. An easy-to-read and pleasantly illustrated retelling of a creation myth. (A-B)

For All Seasons

Blueberries Lavender: Songs of the Farmer's Children, by Nancy Dingman Watson; illus. by Erik Blegvad. Addison. 1977. A collection of poetry depicting seasonal activities of times long ago. The illustrations are set in New England. (A-B)

A Child's Calendar, by John Updike; illus. by Nancy Ekholm Burkert. Knopf, 1965. A poem and its accompanying illustration catch the mood of each month of the year. (A-B)

Four Stories for Four Seasons, by Tomie de Paola. Prentice, 1977. Four friends—Dog, Cat, Frog, and Pig—go in and out of the four seasons, all dressed in Victorian garb. A picture storybook. (A)

I Greet the Dawn: Poems of Paul Laurence Dunbar, sel. and illus. by Ashley Bryan. Atheneum. 1978.   A brief biography together with a selection of this black poet's work.   (B)

Jewish Holidays: Facts, Activities and Crafts, by Susan G. Purdy. Lippincott. 1969.   The history of sixteen major Jewish holidays from ancient times to the present day, together with clear instructions for crafts and activities related to each holiday. A companion volume is *Festivals for You to Celebrate* (Lippincott, 1969).   (C)

O Frabjous Day: Poetry for Holidays and Special Occasions, comp. by Myra Cohn Livingston. A Margaret K. McElderry Book/Atheneum, 1975.   Over one hundred poems celebrating all kinds of holidays as well as days of sorrow, such as the assassinations of Kennedy and King.   (C-D)

Pumpkin in a Pear Tree: Creative Ideas for Twelve Months of Holiday Fun, by Ann Cole and others. Little, 1976. Paper, Little.   Games, crafts, recipes, and decorations for a variety of holidays, both usual and unusual. The instructions are simple and readily adaptable. (B-C)

Songs of the Chippewa, ad. from the collections of Frances Densmore and Henry R. Schoolcraft; arr. for piano and guitar by John Bierhorst; pictures by Joe Servello. Farrar, 1974.   An attractive edition of an old classic which will be enjoyed by a new audience. (B-C)

The Star in the Pail, by David McCord; illus. by Marc Simont. Little, 1975.   A collection of twenty-six poems from this poet's previously published works. Other volumes of his include *All Day Long* (Little, 1966. Paper, Dell/Yearling) and *Take Sky* (Little, 1962). (B-C)

Books for Family Sharing

Fears and Feelings

A Book of Scary Things, by Paul Showers and Susan Perl. Doubleday, 1977.   Practical hints for dealing with real fears and sharing
the scariness of imaginary frights.   (A-B)

Ira Sleeps Over, by Bernard Waber. Houghton, 1972. Paper. Houghton/
Sandpiper.   Ira has a problem. Will Reggie laugh if he brings his
teddy bear when he sleeps over? A picture book filled with understanding and humor.   (A)

*My Mama Says There Aren't Any Zombies, Ghosts, Vampires, Crea-
tures, Demons, Monsters, Fiends, Goblins, or Things,* by Judith
Viorst; illus. by Kay Chorao. Atheneum. 1973. Paper. Atheneum/
Aladdin.   If a mother has made other important mistakes, should a
child believe her now? A fun and contemporary look at an age-old
problem of childhood.   (A-B)

The Quarreling Book, by Charlotte Zolotow; illus. by Arnold Lobel.
Harper, 1963.   On a rainy day, the James family pass along bad and
good feelings. A picture book.   (A)

Will It Be Okay? by Crescent Dragonwagon; illus. by Ben Shecter.
Harper, 1977.   "But what if there is thunder and lightning?" A
fast-thinking mother calmly answers all her timid child's fearful
questions.   (A)

Nursery School

My Nursery School, by Harlow Rockwell. Greenwillow, 1976.
Bright, realistic illustrations and a brief text paint a picture of
happy nursery school activities to give heart to any new scholar.
(A)

Shawn Goes to School, by Petronella Breinburg; illus. by Errol Lloyd. Crowell, 1974.   Simple text and strongly colored illustrations portray apprehensive Shawn's first day at nursery school. (A)

Will I Have a Friend? by Miriam Cohen; illus. by Lillian Hoban. Macmillan, 1967. Paper, Collier/Macmillan.   A reassuring Pa takes Jim to school on that very important first day.

The New Baby

Confessions of an Only Child, by Norma Klein; illus. by Richard Cuffari. Pantheon. 1974. Paper. Dell/Yearling.   Cherished, eight-year-old Toe (Antonia) is not sure she wants to share her comfortable family life until grief and guilt help her to truly welcome baby Brendan.   (B-C)

Dorrie's Book, by Marilyn Sachs; illus. by Anne Sachs. Doubleday, 1975.   Indulged, intelligent "only child" Dorie describes what happens to her family when the new baby is triplets.   (B-C)

Peggy's New Brother, by Eleanor Schick. Macmillan, 1970.   Peggy finds a special something that only she can do for her new brother Peter.   (A)

She Come Bringing Me That Little Baby Girl, by Eloise Greenfield; illus. by John Steptoe. Lippincott, 1974.   Kevin decides he doesn't want to be "a brother to no girls" until he discovers that Uncle Roy is Mama's big brother. Strong illustrations.   (A-B)

Watching the New Baby, by Joan Samson. Atheneum, 1974.   What to anticipate and appreciate as the new baby grows and develops. Illustrated with photographs from real life.   (B-C)

Dentist/Doctor/Hospital

Doctor Shawn, by Petronella Breinburg; illus. by Errol Lloyd. Crowell, 1975.   Big sister is nurse because she "was the doctor last time" as children play hospital while Mom is away.   (A)

Elizabeth Gets Well, by Alfons Weber; illus. by Jacqueline Blass. Crowell, 1970. Paper, Crowell.   A Swiss pediatrician father describes the entire hospitalization, operation, and recovery process for an appendectomy in a factual narrative text supported by cheerful and detailed illustrations.   (A-B)

Jeff's Hospital Book, by Harriet L. Sobol. Walck, 1975.   Jeff is the author's son who really did have his eyes straightened during hospitalization, photographically recorded in this reassuring book. (A-B)

My Dentist, by Harlow Rockwell. Greenwillow, 1975.   The colorful, detailed drawings add realism to this factual, intimate account of a child's trip to the dentist. A companion volume to *My Doctor* (Macmillan, 1973).   (A)

The Sick Book: Questions and Answers about Hiccups and Mumps, Sneezes and Bumps, and Other Things That Go Wrong with Us, by Marie Winn; illus. by Fred Grenner. Four Winds, 1976.   An encyclopedic collection of data about minor and major illnesses, designed to answer the questions of an ill child who is not too sick to read, or of a medically curious, healthy child.   (B)

Moving

The Big Hello, by Janet Schulman; illus. by Lillian Hoban. Greenwillow, 1976.   A little girl finds comfort in her doll as she adjust to a cross-country moving experience. A simple, easy-to-read story. (A)

Moving, by Wendy Watson. Crowell, 1978.   Muffin decides that to be alone in the old house may be worse then being lonely with company in a new house.   (A)

Moving Day, by Tobi Tobias; pictures by William Pène du Bois. Knopf, 1976.   A cheerful view of the many changes moving brings: "new house, new home, good-bye, hello."   (A)

Adoption

Abby, by Jeannette Caines; illus. by Steven Kellogg. Harper, 1973.   An adopted sister is just as pesky as any other sister and just as lovable.   (A)

The Chosen Baby, 3rd ed., by Valentina Wasson; illus. by Glo Coalson. Lippincott, 1977.   A classic picture book which explains adoption and is a companion to the adult book of the same title.   (A)

I Am Adopted, by Susan Lapsley; illus. by Michael Charlton. Bradbury, 1975.   Charles explains why "adoption means belonging." Large print and simple, bright pictures make the book accessible to the youngest sharers.   (A)

Is That Your Sister? A True Story of Adoption, by Catherine and Sherry Bunin. Pantheon, 1976.   Warm, realistic mother-daughter explanation of one family's experience with expansion through adoption. Illustrated with family album photographs.   (B)

Divorce

A Book for Jodan, by Marcia Newfield; illus. by Diane de Groat. A Margaret K. McElderry Book/Atheneum, 1975.   Jodan's father creates a special book for her to help her remember how important they are to each other when they are far apart.   (B)

The Boys and Girls Book about Divorce, with an Introduction for Parents, by Richard A. Gardner; foreword by Louis Bates Ames; illus. by Alfred Lowenheim. Aronson, 1971. Paper, Bantam.   Helpful source of honest, reassuring answers to the myriad of questions which plague children involved in divorce.   (B-C)

Emily and the Klunky Baby and the Next-Door Dog, by Joan M. Lexau; illus. by Martha Alexander. Dial, 1972.   In this small picture book, Emily's Mama is too busy doing things Daddy used to do to give Emily the attention she wants and needs. So, Emily attempts to run away with the klunky baby.   (A)

Me Day, by Joan M. Lexau; pictures by Robert Weaver. Dial. 1971. Deft illustrations reflect the family love which surrounds Rafer on his birthday.   (A)

Out of Love, by Hilma Wolitzer. Farrar, 1976. Paper, Bantam.   How do parents fall "out of love?" Teenage Teddy puzzles this question as she reads her father's old love letters to her divorced mother.   (C-D)

Where Is Daddy? The Story of a Divorce, by Beth Goff; drawings by Susan Perl. Beacon, 1969. As Janeydear hurts and hates, she experiences all the emotions which haunt small children who fear that divorce means losing a parent forever.   (B)

Death

The Accident, by Carol Carrick; illus. by Donald Carrick. Houghton/ Clarion. 1976.   A small boy experiences shock and grief when he witnesses the accidental death of his dog.   (A-B)

Annie and the Old One, by Miska Miles; illus. by Peter Parnall. Atlantic/Little, 1971.   A small Navajo girl cannot imagine life without her grandmother, the Old One; so, by prolonging the weaving of the new rug, she attempts to hold back time.   (B)

Beat The Turtle Drum, by Constance C. Greene; illus. by Donna Diamond. Viking, 1976. Paper. Dell/Yearling.   Two sisters, Kate and Joss, share their joys, but only Kate is left to deal with her sorrow and her parents' grief when Joss falls from the apple tree. (B-C)

The Dead Bird, by Margaret Wise Brown; illus. by Remy Charlip. Addison, 1958. A simple introduction to traditional burial customs, as children bury a bird that was "dead when we found it." (A)

Learning to Say Good-by: When a Parent Dies, by Eda Le Shan; illus. by Paul Giovanopoulos. Macmillan. 1976. Paper. Avon. An honest and sensitive exploration of the grief, fears, and fantasies that a parent's death will bring to a child. (C-D)

Nonna, by Jennifer Bartoli; illus. by Joan Drescher. Harvey, 1974. Mourning and memories are shared by a close-knit family when a beloved grandmother dies. (C-D)

The Sound of Chariots, by Mollie Hunter. Harper, 1972. Paper. Avon. Desperate grief engulfs daredevil Bridie when her adored father dies, but it serves as a stimulus when she sees she must live for him through her poetry. (C)

When People Die, by Joanne E. Bernstein; Stephen V. Gullo. Dutton, 1977. Death as a natural function of life together with a sensitive approach to funeral customs and family sorrow is the major thrust of this informational book. (C-D)

Disabilities

Claire and Emma, by Diana Peter. Day, 1977. Brightly colored photographs illustrate this account of the similiarities to, and differences from, an ordinary child's life as shown in the behavior of two hearing-impaired sisters. British setting and vocabulary. (A-B)

Don't Feel Sorry for Paul, by Bernard Wolf. Lippincott. 1974. Paul Jockimo was born with incompletely formed hands and feet, yet with the aid of prostheses he leads a competitive, athletic, full life, which the reader is privileged to share through the warm, descriptive text and illustrations. Companion volumes are *Anna's Silent World* (Lippincott, 1977) and *Connie's New Eyes* (Lippincott, 1976. Paper, Archway). (A-B)

Howie Helps Himself, by Joan Fassler; pictures by Joe Lasker. Whitman, 1975. Howie tries and tries to move his wheelchair along. He practices, cries, and almost gives up, but one glad, glorious day he shares his success with his father. (A)

I Have a Sister, My Sister Is Deaf; by Jeanne Peterson. Harper, 1977. The pleasures and problems of sharing family life with a sister who watches rather than listens. Illustrated with muted pencil sketches of multiracial children. (A-B)

Karen, by Marie Killilea. Prentice, 1962. Paper, Dell. The biography of a cerebral palsied child, written by her mother who shares her initial despair, constant hope, and eventual triumph. (C-D)

Like Me, by Alan Brightman. Little, 1976. Paper. Little. Photographs of happy, involved children support an explanatory text, in rhyme, that reveals how a mentally retarded youngster looks at himself and his friends. (A-B)

Rachel, by Elizabeth Fanshawe; illus. by Michael Charlton. Bradbury, 1977. Rachel is "in a wheelchair" as she participates fully in school and home activities. (A)

Human Sexuality and Reproduction

The Beauty of Birth, by Colette Portal; ad. from the French by Guy Daniels. Knopf, 1971. Foetal development from the union of sperm and ovum to triumphant birth shown in delicate pastel watercolors. (B-C)

How Babies Are Made, by Andrew C. Andry and Steven Shepp. Time, 1968. Colorful collages and precise text describe reproductive processes in nature: flowers (with bees), poultry, canines, and humans from fertilized egg to birth. (B-C)

How New Life Begins, by Ester Meeks and Elizabeth Bagwell. Follett, 1969. Vivid photographs and concise text detail the development of life in nature. Philosophic, biological approach. (B-C)

Love and Sex in Plain Language, 3rd ed., by Eric W. Johnson; illus. by Edward C. Smith. Lippincott, 1974. Simple, frank discussion for older children, augmented by diagrams and drawings. (D)

We Are Having a Baby, by Vicki Holland. Scribner, 1972. Paper, Scribner. A simple presentation of preschooler Dana's feelings during her mother's pregnancy, hospitalization, and homecoming with a new baby brother. Illustrated with photographs by the author. (A)

Where Do Babies Come From? A Book for Children and Their Parents, by Margaret Sheffield; illus. by Sheila Bewley. Knopf, 1973. The clear, simple text is colorfully and realistically illustrated. Body differences from infancy to maturity are described. (A-C)

Wind Rose, by Crescent Dragonwagon; illus. by Ronald Himler. Harper, 1976. A mother tells her daughter, with great love and tenderness, of her conception, development in the womb, and birth at home. A poetic picture storybook. (B)

The Wonderful Story of How You Were Born, rev. ed., by Sidonie M. Gruenberg; illus. by Symeon Shimin. Doubleday, 1970. Paper, Doubleday. Warm text and beautiful illustrations describe birth, sexual development, the reproductive processes, and the function of various sexual organs. (B)

Activities for Children

The Big Book of Jokes, by Helen Hoke; illus. by Richard Erdoes. Watts, 1971. Old favorites and new absurdities to evoke laughter and response on car trips, at dinner tables, and around campfires. (B)

The Book of Think (or, How to Solve a Problem Twice Your Size), by Marilyn Burns; illus. by Martha Weston. A Brown Paper School Book/Little, 1976. Paper, Little. "Sometimes people say things like this: *It can't be solved. I don't know how. I give up.* That will never do. There is always another way to look at a problem. That's what this book is about: looking at problems and learning to think in new ways." (B-C)

Fun with Pencil and Paper: Games, Stunts, Puzzles, by Joseph Leeming; pictures by Jessie Robinson. Lippincott, 1955. This contains the rules for more than a hundred pencil and paper games, stunts, and puzzles. (B)

Indoor Games and Activities, by Sylvia Cassell. Harper, 1960. Easily followed directions for experiments, puzzles, homecrafts, and arts designed for the family's younger members. (B-C)

Juba This and Juba That, ed. by Virginia A. Tashjian; illus. by Victoria de Lorrea. Little, 1969. "A book of rhymes and songs to sing and play, stories to tell and riddles to guess" can be a great boon to den mothers, storytellers, and campfire leaders. (B)

Let's Do Fingerplays, by Marion Grayson. Luce, 1962. Teachers, mothers, and older brothers and sisters will enjoy using this collection of more than two hundred games, rhymes, and songs with young children. (C-D)

Mr. Mysterious's Secrets of Magic, by Sid Fleischman; illus. by Eric von Schmidt. Atlantic/Little, 1975. Twenty entertaining tricks using inexpensive props. An enjoyable book. (B)

Rainy Day Book, by Alvin Schwartz. Simon, 1968. Paper, Simon/ Fireside. A "survival kit for harassed parents," this contains dramatic and musical activities as well as games, crafts, and science experiments. (C-D)

Recyclopedia: Games, Science Equipment, and Crafts from Recycled Materials, written and illus. by Robin Simons. Houghton, 1976. Paper, Houghton/Sandpiper. A cornucopia of inventive ideas, craft projects, and off-beat sources which originated at the Boston Children's Museum. (B-C)

Riddles of Many Lands, ed. by Carl Withers and Sula Benet; illus. by Lili Cassell. Abelard, 1956. Eight hundred folk riddles arranged by countries, cultures, and tribes. (B)

Tomfoolery: Trickery and Foolery with Words, by Alvin Schwartz; illus. by Glen Rounds. Lippincott, 1973. Paper, Lippincott. An unusually attractive collection, and fun for all. (B)

What? A Riddle Book, by Jane Sarnoff and Reynold Ruffins. Scribner, 1974. Paper, Scribner. The zany illustrations as well as the corny and novel one-line riddles will intrigue young raconteurs and their audiences. (B)

Which One Is Different? by Joel Rothman. Doubleday, 1975. Visual puzzles requiring patience and observational acuity challenge adults and children equally. (B)

Other Resources for Parents' Reading

Books, Children and Men, by Paul Hazard; trans. by Marguerite Mitchell. Horn Book, 1944. Paper, Horn Book.

A Parents' Guide to Children's Reading, 4th ed., by Nancy Larrick. Doubleday, 1975. Paper, Doubleday.

Start Early for an Early Start, ed. by Fern Johnson. Paper, ALA, 1976.

Storytelling: Art and Technique, by Augusta Baker and Ellin Greene. Bowker, 1978. Paper, Bowker.

Publishers and
Their Addresses

Abelard. *see* Crowell Junior Books.

Abingdon. Abingdon Press, 201 Eighth Ave. S, Nashville, TN 37202

Ace. Ace Books, 360 Park Ave. S, New York, NY 10010

Addison. Addison-Wesley Publishing Co., Inc., Jacob Way, Reading, MA 01867

Airmont. Airmont Books, 22 E. 60th St., New York, NY 10022

ALA. American Library Association, 50 E. Huron St., Chicago, IL 60611

Apollo. Apollo Editions, 10 E. 53rd St., New York, NY 10022

Archway. Archway Press, Inc., 48 W. 48th St., New York, NY 10036

Aronson. Jason Aronson, Inc., 111 Eighth Ave., New York, NY 10011

Astor. Astor-Honor, Inc., 48 E. 43rd St., New York, NY 10017

Atheneum. Atheneum Publishers, 597 Fifth Ave., New York, NY 10017

Atlantic/Little. *see* Little, Brown & Co.

Avon. Avon Books, 959 Eighth Ave., New York, NY 10019

BJ. BJ Publishing Group, 200 Madison Ave., New York, NY 10016

Ballantine. Ballantine Books, Inc., 201 E. 50th St., New York, NY 10022

Bantam. Bantam Books, 666 Fifth Ave., New York, NY 10019

Beacon. Beacon Press, 25 Beacon St., Boston, MA 02108

Bobbs. Bobbs-Merrill Co., Inc., 4300 W. 62nd St., Indianapolis, IN 46206

Bonim. Bonim Books, 80 Fifth Ave., New York, NY 10011

Bookstore Pr. Bookstore Press, distr. by Cumberland Press/Bond Wheelwright Co., Box 296, Freeport, ME 04032

Bowker. R. R. Bowker and Co., 1180 Avenue of the Americas, New York, NY 10036

Bradbury. Bradbury Press, Inc., 2 Overhill Rd., Scarsdale, NY 10583

British. British Book Centre, Fairview Park, Elmsford, NY 10523

Brown. William C. Brown Co. Publishers, 2460 Kerper Blvd., Dubuque, IA 52001

Brown Paper School Book. *see* Little, Brown & Co.

Childrens. Childrens Press, Inc. 1224 W. Van Buren St., Chicago, IL 60607

Clarion. *see* Houghton Mifflin/Clarion Books.

Collier/Macmillan. *see* The Macmillan Company.

Collins. *see* Philomel Books.

Contemporary. Contemporary Books, Inc., 180 N. Michigan Ave., Chicago, IL 60601.

Coward. Coward, McCann & Geoghegan, Inc., 200 Madison Ave., New York, NY 10016.

Crowell. Crowell Junior Books, 10 E. 53rd St., New York, NY 10022

Crown. Crown Publishers, Inc., One Park Ave., New York, NY 10016

Daw Books. *see* New American Library.

Day. *see* Crowell Junior Books.

Delacorte. Delacorte Press, 245 E. 47th St., New York, NY 10017

Dell. Dell Publishing Co., Inc. 245 E. 47th St., New York, NY 10017

Dial. The Dial Press, 245 E. 47th St., New York, NY 10017

Dodd. Dodd, Mead & Co., Inc., 79 Madison Ave., New York, NY 10016

Doubleday. Doubleday & Co., Inc., 245 Park Ave., New York, NY 10017

Dover. Dover Publications, Inc., 180 Varick St., New York, NY 10014

Dutton. E. P. Dutton, 2 Park Ave., New York, NY 10016

Elsevier/Nelson Books, 2 Park Ave., New York, NY 10016

Farrar. Farrar, Straus & Giroux, Inc., 19 Union Square W, New York, NY 10003

Follett. Follett Publishing Co., 1010 W. Washington Blvd., Chicago, IL 60607

Four Winds. Four Winds Press, 50 W. 44th St., New York, NY 10036

Golden Gate. *see* Childrens Press.

Greenwillow. Greenwillow Books, 105 Madison Ave., New York, NY 10016

Grosset. Grosset & Dunlap, Inc., 51 Madison Ave., New York, NY 10010

Harcourt. Harcourt Brace Jovanovich, Inc., 757 Third Ave., New York, NY 10017

Harper. Harper & Row, Publishers, Inc., 10 E. 53rd St., New York, NY 10022

Harvey. Harvey House, 20 Waterside Plaza, New York, NY 10010

Hawthorn. Hawthorn Books, Inc., 260 Madison Ave., New York, NY 10016

Hill. Hill & Wang, Inc., 19 Union Square W., New York, NY 10003

Holiday. Holiday House, 18 E. 53rd St., New York, NY 10022

Holt. Holt, Rinehart & Winston, 383 Madison Ave., New York, NY 10017

Horn Book. The Horn Book, Inc., Park Square Bldg., 31 St. James Ave., Boston, MA 02116

Houghton. Houghton Mifflin Co., 2 Park St., Boston, MA 02107

Houghton/Clarion. Houghton Mifflin/Clarion Books, 52 Vanderbilt Ave., New York, NY 10017

Indiana. Indiana University Press, Tenth and Morton Sts., Bloomington, IN 47405

Knopf. Alfred A. Knopf, Inc., 201 E. 50th St., New York, NY 10022

Lawrence, Seymour. *see* Delacorte.

Lippincott. Lippincott Junior Books, 10 E. 53rd St., New York, NY 10022

Little. Little, Brown & Co., 34 Beacon St., Boston, MA 02106

Lollipop Power. Lollipop Power, Inc., PO Box 1171, Chapel Hill, NC 27514

Lothrop. Lothrop, Lee & Shepard Co., 105 Madison Ave., New York, NY 10016

Luce. Robert B. Luce, Inc., 6919 Radnor Rd., Bethesda, MD 20034

McGraw. McGraw-Hill Book Co., 1221 Avenue of the Americas, New York, NY 10020

McKay. David McKay Co., Inc., 2 Park Ave., New York, NY 10016

Macmillan. The Macmillan Publishing Co., Inc., 866 Third Ave., New York, NY 10022

Morrow. William Morrow & Co., Inc., 105 Madison Ave., New York, NY 10016

Nelson. *see* Elsevier/Nelson Books.

New American Library. The New American Library, Inc., 1633 Broadway, New York, NY 10019

New Directions. New Directions Publishing Corp., 80 Eighth Ave., New York, NY 10011

Oxford. Oxford University Press, 200 Madison Ave., New York, NY 10016

Pantheon. Pantheon Books, 201 E. 50th St., New York, NY 10022

Parents. Parents' Magazine Press, 52 Vanderbilt Ave., New York, NY 10017

Parnassus. *see* Houghton Mifflin Co.

Penguin. Penguin Books, 625 Madison Ave., New York, NY 10022

Phillips. S. G. Phillips, Inc., 305 W. 86th St., New York, NY 10024

Philomel. Philomel Books, 200 Madison Ave., New York, NY 10016

Platt. Platt & Munk, Inc., 1055 Bronx River Ave., Bronx, NY 10472

Pocket Books. Pocket Books, 1230 Avenue of the Americas, New York, NY 10020

Prentice. Prentice-Hall, Inc., Englewood Cliffs, NJ 07632

Putnam. G. P. Putnam's Sons, 200 Madison Ave., New York, NY 10016

Pyramid. Pyramid Books, 133 W. 72nd St., New York, NY 10023

Rand. Rand McNally & Co., 8255 Central Park Ave., Skokie, IL 60076

Random. Random House, Inc., 201 E. 50th St., New York, NY 10022

Reilly. Reilly & Lee Books. *see* Contemporary/Books.

Scholastic. Scholastic Book Services, 50 W. 44th St., New York, NY 10036

Scribner. Charles Scribner's Sons, 597 Fifth Ave, New York, NY 10017

Seabury. *see* Houghton Mifflin/Clarion Books.

Sierra Club. *see* Scribner.

Simon. Simon & Schuster, Inc., 1230 Avenue of the Americas, New York, NY 10020

Sniffen Court. *see* Atheneum.

Time. Time-Life Books, Inc., Alexandria, VA 22314

Tundra. Tundra Books. *see* Scribner.

Vanguard. Vanguard Press, Inc., 424 Madison Ave., New York, NY 10017

Viking. Viking Penguin, Inc., 625 Madison Ave., New York, NY 10022

UNICEF. U.S. Committee for UNICEF, 331 E. 38th St., New York, NY 10016

Walck. Henry Z. Walck, Inc., 2 Park Ave., New York, NY 10016

Walker. Walker & Company, 720 Fifth Ave., New York, NY 10019

Warne. Frederick Warne Co., Inc., 2 Park Ave., New York, NY 10016

Watts. Franklin Watts, Inc., 730 Fifth Ave., New York, NY 10019

Weatherhill. John Weatherhill, Inc., 149 Madison Ave., New York, NY 10016

Westminster. The Westminster Press, 925 Chestnut St., Philadelphia, PA 19107

Whitman. Albert Whitman & Co., 560 W. Lake St., Chicago, IL 60606

Windmill. Windmill Books, Inc., 1230 Avenue of the Americas, New York, NY 10020

World. *see* Philomel Books.

Author–Title Index

Index compiled by Sandi Schroeder.

Designed by Vladimir Reichl
Composed in Mergenthaler CRTronic Melior
   by Imperial Printing Company
Printed on Antique Glatfelter, a
   pH-neutral stock, and bound by
   the University of Chicago Printing Deparment
Cover design and art by Melissa Woodburn